The Glocalization of Shanghai Disneyland

Focusing on Disney's production of Shanghai Disneyland, this book examines how the Chinese state and the local market influence Disney's ownership and production of the identities and the representations of Shanghai Disneyland. Qualitative methods are here applied to combine both primary and secondary data, including document analysis, participant observation, and in-depth interviews.

Shanghai Disneyland is purposely created to be different from the other Disneylands, under the "authentically Disney and distinctly Chinese" mandate. In order to survive and thrive in China, Disney carefully constructs Shanghai Disneyland as Disneyland with Chinese characteristics. Previous studies tend to link Disney with cultural imperialism; however, this book argues that it is not imperialism but glocalization that promotes a global company's interests in China. In particular, the findings suggest state-capital-led glocalization: glocalization led by economic capital *of* the state (direct investment) and economic capital *with* the state (market potential). Furthermore, the four categories of glocalization with different conditions, considerations, and consequences illustrate various global–local dynamics in the process of a global formation of locality.

The Glocalization of Shanghai Disneyland will appeal to students and scholars of sociology, communication studies, business studies, and Asian studies more broadly.

Ni-Chen Sung is experienced in the entertainment industry across the region. With The Walt Disney Company, she was head of creative in Taiwan, and director of production in China. Dr. Sung has research interests in globalization and the cultural industries.

Routledge Focus on Asia

1. **The Abe Administration and Rise of the Prime Ministerial Executive**
   Aurelia George Mulgan

2. **Heritage Revitalisation for Tourism in Hong Kong**
   The Role of Interpretative Planning
   Chris White

3. **Prisons and Forced Labour in Japan**
   The Colonization of Hokkaido, 1881-1894
   Pia Maria Jolliffe

4. **Chaoxianzu Entrepreneurs in Korea**
   Searching for Citizenship in the Ethnic Homeland
   Park Woo

5. **The Glocalization of Shanghai Disneyland**
   Ni-Chen Sung

The Glocalization of Shanghai Disneyland

Ni-Chen Sung

LONDON AND NEW YORK

First published 2021
by Routledge
2 Park Square, Milton Park, Abingdon, Oxon OX14 4RN

and by Routledge
605 Third Avenue, New York, NY 10158

Routledge is an imprint of the Taylor & Francis Group, an informa business

© 2021 Ni-Chen Sung

The right of Ni-Chen Sung to be identified as author of this work has been asserted by her in accordance with sections 77 and 78 of the Copyright, Designs and Patents Act 1988.

All rights reserved. No part of this book may be reprinted or reproduced or utilised in any form or by any electronic, mechanical, or other means, now known or hereafter invented, including photocopying and recording, or in any information storage or retrieval system, without permission in writing from the publishers.

Trademark notice: Product or corporate names may be trademarks or registered trademarks, and are used only for identification and explanation without intent to infringe.

British Library Cataloguing-in-Publication Data
A catalogue record for this book is available from the British Library

Library of Congress Cataloging-in-Publication Data
A catalog record has been requested for this book

ISBN: 978-0-367-67550-9 (hbk)
ISBN: 978-0-367-67588-2 (pbk)
ISBN: 978-1-003-13190-8 (ebk)

Typeset in Times New Roman
by SPi Global, India

Contents

	List of figures	vi
	List of tables	vii
	Acknowledgments	viii
	Author biography	ix
1	Introduction	1
2	Histories of Disney	8
3	Ownership structure of Shanghai Disneyland	28
4	Construction of local identities for Shanghai Disneyland	45
5	"Distinctly Chinese" representations of Shanghai Disneyland	65
6	Implications of the differences of Shanghai Disneyland	83
	Index	96

Figures

1.1	Analytical framework and organization of the book	5
5.1	Themed lands at Shanghai Disneyland	66
6.1	Production's relationships with state, market, park identity, and park representation in the case of Shanghai Disneyland	84
6.2	Dual encodings of "state-capital" in the concept of *state-capital-led glocalization* and respective outputs in the case of Shanghai Disneyland	88
6.3	The approach of political economy of communication and Shanghai Disneyland	90
6.4	Four categories of glocalization	92

Tables

1.1	Disneyland and the opening dates	2
3.1	Ownership structure of Shanghai Disneyland	28
3.2	Disney's ownership in Disneyland outside of the United States	31
4.1	Identity of Disneyland outside of the United States	46
5.1	Dual encodings of the "distinctly Chinese" discourse for Shanghai Disneyland	76
6.1	Four categories of glocalization	94

Acknowledgments

Experienced in the industry yet young in the academia, I would not have started this project without solid academic training at The Chinese University of Hong Kong. First, I would like to thank Professor Anthony Fung, who helped me coin the term, state-capital-led glocalization, while I worked on my doctoral thesis. Deep gratitude to Professor Joseph Chan and Professor Jack Qiu who led me through the broad literature on cultural globalization. My sincere thanks to Professor Ven-hwei Lo, Professor Paul Lee, and Professor Eric Ma who encouraged me to believe in myself, keep thinking, and follow my dreams.

I am grateful for my time with Disney. To some extent, this is a reflexive study to decode my over-one-decade working experiences across the region with the company. My unfeigned thanks to my Disney informants and friends who shared their wisdom. I am also thankful to my former team members who flew to Hong Kong for a surprise Christmas dinner to wish me the very best on my research.

Finalizing this book during the 2020 global pandemic helped alleviate anxiety. When I clarified my thoughts by virtue of writing, there existed hopes to generate humble knowledge for a better understanding of the world. Heartfelt thanks to my Routledge contacts who made this quest possible. My genuine thanks to Stephanie who recognized this project and facilitated the greenlight. My thanks also go to Emily and Balambigai who shared the know-hows for publication.

Profound gratitude to my family who taught me the values of integrity, curiosity, and diversity. I owe a debt of gratitude to my mom who gave me the strength to leave my comfort zone. She is now in Heaven but love will never end. Special thanks to my spiritual mentor, Master Sheng-Yen. This book witnesses the power of faith.

Author biography

Dr. Ni-Chen Sung received her Bachelor's Degree in Sociology from National Taiwan University, Master's Degree in TV-Radio-Film from Syracuse University in the United States, and PhD Degree in Communication from The Chinese University of Hong Kong and has research interests in globalization, film studies, and the cultural industries. New in the academia but experienced in the industry, Dr. Sung has nearly two decades of regional experiences in the entertainment industry. With The Walt Disney Company, she was award-winning writer/producer in Singapore, head of creative in Taiwan, and director of production in Beijing and Shanghai. She also worked on some projects with Singapore's MediaCorp Channel 8 and Discovery Networks. Dr. Sung aims to leverage industry experiences and academic studies to generate humble knowledge for a better understanding of the world.

1 Introduction

Background

My initial interest in this project is out of imagination, which I believe is not less important than knowledge. Once in a while, I imagined China as Disneyland, with the death penalty, for a few reasons. First, almost every child in China is raised like a princess or a prince under the one-child policy, in effect from 1979 to 2015. Second, the Chinese party–state's emphasis on "harmonious society," proposed by former President Hu Jintao, resonates with the so-called Disneyfication (Schickel, 1997) to clean up the unpleasant past. Third, the launch of Hong Kong Disneyland before the spotlighted Shanghai Disneyland echoes the Chinese government's preference for a pilot before the official launch of a policy.

Furthermore, Disney did not seem to be an evil empire to China in my experience. When I worked on *Jia Pian You Yue*, which introduced Disney's animated features on China Central Television's Movie Channel (CCTV6), my co-workers from both sides of Disney and CCTV6 warned me to pay great attention to the differences between capitalist Disney and socialist China. "Watch out for the landmines along the way," Mr. Li, a benign department head from CCTV6 constantly reminded me. However, I observed more similarities than differences between the practices in place at Disney and CCTV6. For example, Chinese television forbids the portrayal of high school students wearing earrings, revealing clothing, or with dyed hair, which was entirely consistent with Disney's production guidelines I had been following for years.

Sometimes, Disney's production guidelines appeared stricter than local Chinese practices. According to Disney's standards and practices for media production, a character must wear a seatbelt when driving a car, passengers need to wear life jackets when taking a boat ride and must keep their hands inside the boat, and no junk food can be featured in the program or advertisement in keeping with Disney's healthy food guidelines (Gao, 2016). Contrary to the general assumption that the relationship between Disney and CCTV6 is ambivalent, Disney harmonizes surprisingly well with contemporary socialism with Chinese characteristics. Such "harmony" makes it appealing to study Disneyland, "the happiest place on Earth," in the context of China.

To enjoy Disneyland to the fullest, visitors are supposed to be familiar with Disney characters and stories (Lee & Fung, 2013). In the international markets, Disney has often promoted its merchandise and content, including Disneyland, through Disney Channel ever since the channel's international debut in 1995, in Taiwan. However, Disney Channel is unlikely to be approved for broadcast in highly controlled China. Consequently, Shanghai Disneyland has become the company's engine to drive Disney's brand awareness and brand affinity for its other lines of business. In Disney's earnings report for the fiscal year 2016 (from October 2015 to September 2016), the "Parks and Resorts" section reported a decrease in the operating income at the operations outside of the United States due to lower attendance at both Disneyland Paris and Hong Kong Disneyland. Such a decrease was partially offset by the benefit of the first full quarter of operations for Shanghai Disneyland. In just a few months, Shanghai Disneyland had proved its ability to generate revenue as an important strategic asset.

All in all, the fact that two Disney parks are operating in China is noteworthy. There are six Disneyland in the world: two in the United States, one in Japan, one in Paris, and two in China, including Hong Kong Disneyland and Shanghai Disneyland (Table 1.1). Such a weight on China makes the conditions, changes, and consequences of Shanghai Disneyland intriguing for study. Furthermore, contrary to the other Disneyland outside of the United States concluded as "not differ dramatically from the American ones as the company is not keen on investing in creating new concepts" because of the belief that "the

Table 1.1 Disneyland and the opening dates

Park	Opening date
Disneyland Anaheim, California, USA	July 17, 1955
Walt Disney World, Florida, USA	October 1, 1971
Tokyo Disneyland, Japan	April 15, 1983
Disneyland Paris, France	April 12, 1992
Hong Kong Disneyland, China	September 12, 2005
Shanghai Disneyland, China	June 16, 2016

attraction of Disneyland is its faithfulness to the original Disneyland in California" (Lee & Fung, 2013: 45), Shanghai Disneyland is purposely created to be different from the other Disneyland under the creative direction of being "authentically Disney and distinctly Chinese." This unusual mandate further triggered my interest in studying for what reasons, in which ways, and with what implications Shanghai Disneyland is different from the other Disneyland.

Among Walt Disney's contributions to American popular culture, his theme parks attracted special attention (Wilson, 1993). In Walt's view, "Disneyland is the star. Everything else (in the company) is in the supporting role" (Smith, 2001: 62). Nowadays, the Walt Disney Company has four main business segments: Media Networks; Disney Parks, Experiences and Products; Studio Entertainment; and Direct-to-Consumer and International. Because my over-one-decade working experience with Disney is limited in the Media Networks division: in Singapore as writer/producer, in Taiwan as head of creative, and in Beijing and Shanghai as director of production, studying unfamiliar parks business helps me keep a critical distance from my research topic. To develop a comprehensive understanding of the production of Shanghai Disneyland, various qualitative methods were applied to combine both primary and secondary data, including document analysis, participant observation, and in-depth interviews.

As Wasko advised, documents were crucial for production studies as it was difficult in getting access to interview producers (Lent & Amazeen, 2015). To study Disney, Wasko encouraged researchers to analyze public documents instead of asking for permissions to access Disney archives, since there was enough in public about Disney. In addition to document analysis, this book has benefitted from in-depth interviews. I interviewed 23 Disney's executives in Shanghai, Beijing, and Hong Kong from various lines of business. The average interview time was one hour. When the interviews were conducted, 17 of my informants were present Disney staff and six of them were former employees. Five of them were senior managers and 18 informants were at the director level or above. My informants provided a comprehensive understanding of the company's business, which was crucial to study Disneyland, as Disney's earlier practices in China informed the later comer of Shanghai Disneyland. Although Disney was criticized as an incredible example of corporate enclosure of culture which is extreme in terms of its control (Wasko, 2016, Wilson, 1993), all my interviewees were very open to me. Almost every interview ended with my informant's warm invitation of "contact me any time if you have any further questions."

It is no secret that there is a standard non-disclosure agreement in Disney's employment agreements, which requests its employees to follow the confidentiality terms. For both ethical and legal reasons, all data analyzed in this book are published or interview materials; there is no confidential business information I obtained when I worked with the company. Overall, my time with Disney makes two major contributions to this study. First, it allows me precious access to interview Disney's executives, which helps me with an extensive and original understanding of the company's practices in China. Second, my comprehension of Disney's company culture grants me a stronger position to interpret the data collected.

To analyze Shanghai Disneyland, I borrow the elements in the circuit of culture (Du Gay et al., 1997). One original element, regulation, is replaced in this study by "state" because, in China, the party–state can override legal decisions and make law-like rules. Consumption is replaced by "market" because this is a production study and the production of Shanghai Disneyland prior to any consumption is influenced by local market research. In other words, the elements analyzed in this study are *production*, *state*, *market*, park *identity*, and park *representation* (Figure 1.1). That is, focusing on Disney's production of Shanghai Disneyland, this book examines how the Chinese state and the local market influence Disney's ownership and production of the identities and the representations of Shanghai Disneyland.

Book structure

As illustrated in Figure 1.1, this book is organized into six chapters, around three keywords: Disney, China, and globalization. Following this chapter of "Introduction," which introduces the research background and organization of the book, Chapter Two studies Disney's histories in the United States and in China to build a solid foundation for the examination of Disney's production of Shanghai Disneyland. Chapter Two first reviews how Disney Brothers Cartoon Studio evolved into The Walt Disney Company, followed by the histories of Disney's business in China, including The Walt Disney Company (China) Ltd., Hong Kong Disneyland, and Shanghai Disneyland from the parks' negotiations to the openings.

Chapter Three turns to production's relationship with the Chinese state and regulations through the analysis of the ownership structure of Shanghai Disneyland. Regulated by China's *Catalogue for the Guidance of Foreign Investment Industries*, Disney formed a joint

Introduction 5

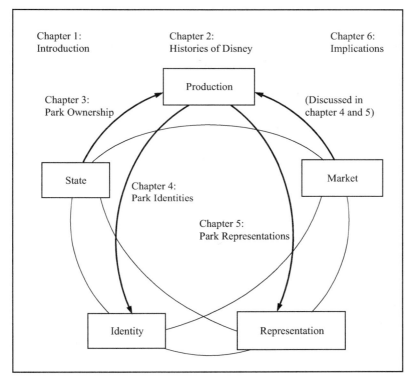

Figure 1.1 Analytical framework and organization of the book

venture with the state-owned Shanghai Shendi Group for Shanghai Disneyland. In the ownership companies of this joint venture, Disney owns a minority of 43 percent of the park's shares due to the majority Chinese ownership rule. In the management company, Disney owns 70 percent of the interests in exchange for management fees and, more importantly, for government relations through sharing the company's theme-park management expertise for the development of local tourism industry, an agenda promoted by the Chinese party–state. Such special arrangements indicate a transformation of the traditional central–peripheral roles while non-Western countries are gradually empowered by economic prosperity. It is not imperialism but glocalization that promotes a global company's interests in China. In particular, the ownership structure of Shanghai Disneyland suggests *state-capital-led glocalization*: glocalization led by economic capital *of* the state (direct investment) and economic capital *with* the state (market potential).

6 *Introduction*

Chapter Four focuses on production's relationship with the park's identity. Unlike the other Disneyland, Disney purposely constructed local identities for "distinctly Chinese" Shanghai Disneyland as "China's Disneyland" and "a citizen of Shanghai." In China, localization is an important strategy for Disney to win the entrée. Back in 2005, The Walt Disney Company (China) Ltd. was coined as "The Chinese Walt Disney Company" to promote its business through local partnership and stratified localization. Local identities for Shanghai Disneyland and Disney's other lines of business in China serve to avoid the social critics of cultural imperialism, in addition to increasing local audience relevance. In the case of Disney's business in China, capitalism appears to thrive in the contradictory direction of imperialist homogenized global culture. The findings suggest a reorientation of the cultural imperialism tradition.

Chapter Five examines production's relationship with the park's representations. This chapter first conducts a descriptive examination of the park's representations through the exclusion and inclusion of the themed lands, attractions, and entertainment performances, followed by an analytical study of the "distinctly Chinese" discourse. The exclusion of iconic Disneyland attractions indicates an effort to avoid an impression of cultural imperialism. The inclusion proposes a discourse of the "distinctly Chinese" representations, which attends to both Chinese cultural references and contemporary Chinese preferences of uniqueness and technological advances. Both the exclusion and the inclusion resonate with the China Dream thesis the Chinese President Xi Jinping proposed and suggest the predominance of the Chinese party–state in the production of Shanghai Disneyland.

Chapter Six recaps the major findings of this study and discusses the implications of the differences of Shanghai Disneyland. According to Walt Disney, "Disneyland will never be completed. It will continue to grow as long as there is imagination left in the world (Smith, 2001: 61)." Previous studies on Disney often raised concerns about the empire's cultural imperialism (Dorfman & Mattelart, 1971; Schiller, 1991). However, the ownership structure, identities, and representations of Shanghai Disneyland demonstrate glocalization, in which the global and the local thrive together, as Robertson (1992) proposed. In particular, the production of Shanghai Disneyland suggests state-capital-led glocalization: glocalization led by economic capital *of* the state and economic capital *with* the state, for which a global cultural company is willing to compromise and share its cultural capital in exchange for potential economic returns. The finding of state-capital-led glocalization leads to the discussion of the typology of glocalization. With different conditions, considerations, and consequences, the four categories of glocalization illustrate various global–local dynamics in the process of a global formation of locality when the local meets the global.

Bibliography

Dorfman, A. & Mattelart, A. (1971). *How to read Donald Duck: Imperialist ideology in the Disney comic*. Trans. D. Kunzle, New York: International General.

Du Gay, P., Hall, S., Negus, K. Mackay, H. & Janes, L. (1997). *Doing cultural studies: The story of the Sony Walkman*. London: SAGE Publications Ltd.

Gao, C.L. (2016). SARFT 'diagnoses' children's programs. Gao Chang Li proposes '8 keys' (in Chinese). *Guang Dian Shi Ping*. Retrieved January 8, 2020, from https://chuansongme.com/n/1048245252966.

Lee, M. & Fung, A. (2013). One region, two modernities: Disneyland in Tokyo and Hong Kong. In Anthony Y.H. Fung (Ed.), *Asian popular culture: The global (dis)continuity*, 42–58. New York: Routledge.

Lent, J. & Amazeen, M. (2015). *Key thinkers in critical communication scholarship: From the pioneers to the next generation*. New York: Palgrave Macmillan.

Robertson, R. (1992). *Globalization: Social theory and global culture*. London: SAGE Publications Ltd.

Schiller, H. (1991). Not yet the post-imperialism era. *Critical Studies in Mass Communication*, *8*(1), 13–28.

Schickel, R. (1997). *The Disney version: The life, times, art and commerce of Walt Disney*. Chicago: Ivan R. Dee, Inc.

Smith, D. (2001). *The quotable Walt Disney*. New York: Disney Editions.

Wasko, J. (2016). The political economy of media as a critical approach. *Communication & Society*, *35*, 1–25.

Wilson, A. (1993). Technological utopias. *South Atlantic Quarterly*, *92*(1), 157–173.

2 Histories of Disney

Cultural companies are subject to a process of continuous development which constantly constitutes corporate practices. To better understand Disney's production of Shanghai Disneyland, this chapter examines the company's histories. I will first review how Disney evolved from Disney Brothers Cartoon Studio to The Walt Disney Company, followed by how The Walt Disney Company in China was transformed to "The Chinese Walt Disney Company." I will also introduce the making of Hong Kong Disneyland, which started construction in January 2003 and opened on September 12, 2005, and that of Shanghai Disneyland, which broke ground in April 2011 and opened on June 16, 2016.

Disney Brothers Cartoon Studio and Walt Disney Studios

In 1923, Walt and Roy Disney formed the Disney Brothers Cartoon Studio in the back half of a real estate office on Kingswell Avenue in Hollywood, California. It was renamed to Walt Disney Studios in 1926 and moved to Hyperion Avenue when the company signed a contract with a New York distributor, M.J. Winkler, on October 16th to distribute *Alice Comedies*, based on a cartoon Walt Disney had made before he moved to California from Kansas City (Lee & Madej, 2012). In 1927, Walt Disney Studios created a new character, Oswald the Lucky Rabbit. After making the first year of 26 Oswald cartoons, Walt realized that it was the distributor, not him, who owned the rights. From then on, the company has been extremely cautious about the copyright protection of its intellectual properties. When the business fortunes of the Disney brothers were at their lowest ebb after the Oswald incident, the birth of Mickey Mouse on a train ride from Manhattan to Hollywood freed the brothers of immediate worry, resulting in Walt's famous quote, "It was all started by a mouse" (Smith, 2001: 41).

The early days of Disney were mainly about animated films. On November 18, 1928, the first Mickey Mouse sound film, *Steamboat Willie*, premiered at the Colony Theater in New York. Disney's first full-color animated short, *The Silly Symphony Flowers and Trees*, which premiered at Hollywood Grauman's Chinese Theatre, won Disney's first Academy Award for Best Cartoon in 1932, the first year the Academy started this category. For the rest of that decade, Disney won the Academy's Best Cartoon every year and gained a reputation for quality storytelling and technological advancement. Disney's animations gained popularity in the movie industry, and Walt realized that merchandising the animated characters was an additional source of revenue for the Studios after a New York businessman offered him US$300 for the license to put Mickey Mouse on pencil tablets. Since then, consumer products have been one of the company's priorities.

In 1933, Disney published the first issue of *Mickey Mouse Magazine*. In the same year, the animated short *The Three Little Pigs* was a success, as it arrived at the right national psychological moment, when people were talking about keeping the wolf (the Depression) from the door. In 1937, *Snow White and the Seven Dwarfs* (*Snow White*), Disney's first feature-length animated film, premiered in Hollywood. This movie was the biggest hit in the year 1938. For a brief time, *Snow White* stood as the highest-grossing film in Hollywood history until it was surpassed by the 1939 classic *Gone with the Wind*. Walt believed that short cartoons paid the bills, but after the success of *Snow White*, he felt that future profits were in feature films. Consequently, Disney invested a large amount of time and budget in animated features.

Not long after the initial golden age highlighted by the unexpected financial success of *Snow White*, Walt Disney Studios was surprisingly on the edge of extinction from investing too much money into two animated features, *Pinocchio* and *Fantasia*. Both movies were released in 1940, but neither performed well enough to cover their costs. Disney learned the risks of big investment and made *Dumbo* in 1941 with a limited budget. However, *Bambi*, in 1942, was another expensive film due to Walt's obsession with perfection. In 1941 and 1942, the company lost a total of one million dollars and started to retrench. A bitter strike, which Walt Disney considered a communist plot to sabotage the country (Wallace, 1985), broke out in 1941 when Disney's young employees were not given full credits. The company was completely shut down for a few months due to this strike.

To some extent, World War II saved the Walt Disney Studios. The U.S. government needed an ambassador of good will, and Disney offered an adored name with the company's achievement in animation. During the war, the U.S. government offered Disney substantial precious access to chemicals for filmmaking when it contracted film projects to Disney, such as *Saludos Amigos* (1942) and *The Three Caballeros* (1944) under the government's South American "Good Neighbor" policy (Harrington, 2015). At that time, Disney serviced the departments of Treasury, Agriculture and State, and Army and Navy to produce films for training and propaganda. By the end of the War, Disney had cut its debt to less than three hundred thousand dollars. However, Disney had difficulty regaining its pre-war status as the entertainment market was changing. Unlike the pre-war high-budget films, post-war Disney productions were low-cost package feature films that contained groups of short cartoons, as well as live-action films, such as *Song of the South* (1946) and *So Dear to My Heart* (1948), that were blended with animated segments. In this period, the storytelling conveyed the conventional Disney narrative of the triumph of the weak over the strong, but the subordinated portrayal of African Americans turned controversial (Watts, 2001). Meanwhile, Disney started a low-budget but award-winning, high-return True-Life Adventure series featuring nature photography to revitalize the company.

In 1950, Disney's first completely live-action film *Treasure Island* and animated feature *Cinderella* created another golden era for Disney. Walt Disney believed that entertainment in its broadest sense had become a necessity rather than a luxury. In the 1950s and 1960s, Americans' per capita incomes were higher, and leisure time was increased. The first Disneyland, built in 1955, soon became the star cash machine for the company. It transformed the company from a simple niche moviemaker to a corporate giant who plays a core role in American popular culture.

Taking advantage of cross-platform efficacy, Disneyland's establishment was largely promoted by television, "an open sesame to many things" to Walt Disney (Smith, 2001: 221), who fully exploited the new medium. On Christmas day in 1950, Walt Disney had his television debut in a National Broadcasting Company (NBC) special *One Hour in Wonderland*, which featured a fusion of animation and live-action. Two years later in 1952, Walt established Disneyland Incorporated to secure investment. One-third of its shares were from ABC-Paramount in return for a weekly one-hour television program featuring Disney films and television productions. In 1954, the weekly *Disneyland* television show, hosted by Walt Disney, premiered on the American

Broadcasting Company (ABC) television network to warm up for the opening of Disneyland. By 1961, this series had moved to NBC and was renamed to *Disney's Wonderful World of Color*. The *Disneyland* series eventually ran on all three networks of ABC, NBC, and Columbia Broadcasting System (CBS) under six title changes, but it remained on the air for 29 years. Another popular children's television series, *The Mickey Mouse Club*, debuted in 1955. This variety show transformed girls and boys next-door to young Mouseketeer celebrities, such as Britney Spears and Justin Timberlake.

By making television and film spatial, Disneyland inaugurated a new form of cultural experiential product which created a new opportunity to recycle and cross-promote the company's entire collection of imagery products (Davis, 1996). The first Disneyland opened on July 17, 1955, in Anaheim, California. A 90-minute ABC TV special, featuring celebrities guided by Walt Disney at the park, was broadcast on the day. On Disney's company website, the genesis of Disneyland is described as Walt Disney's intention to build a park "where parents and children could have fun together, unlike the carnivals that he could only see his two young daughters play."

Walt Disney is perceived as a man good at filling conduits with Disneyness and hyper-cleanliness to exclude competition (Gitlin, 2001). When being asked why he wanted to build another amusement park, Walt said that amusement parks were so dirty, but that "mine wouldn't be (Smith, 2001: 47) ... I don't want the public to see the real world they live in while they are in the park... I want them to feel they are in another world" (Smith, 2001: 59). Disneyland was promoted as "the first to use visually compatible elements working as a coordinating theme avoiding the contradictory 'hodgepodge' of World's Fairs and amusement parks" (Gottdiner, 1982: 154). In sum, Walt Disney's idea of Disneyland featured a harmonious and happy-past image from the carnivals Walt remembered from his youth. For example, Main Street USA was said to be fashioned out of Walt's embodied remembrances of his childhood in Marceline, Missouri, a small town about a hundred miles northeast of Kansas City, to bring back memories of the carefree times.

In 1965, Walt Disney began to plan a second theme park with the purchase of 27,400 acres of reclaimed swampland in Florida. One year later, on December 15, 1966, Walt Disney died of lung cancer at age 65 without getting to see the opening of his treasured Magic Kingdom Park at Walt Disney World Resort, which opened on October 1, 1971 in Orlando, Florida. After Walt passed away, the position of chairman was assigned to his brother Roy Disney to lead the 4,000 employees in the way Walt Disney has established and guided. From 1966, when Roy

Disney took over the chairman position, to 1971, when he passed away on December 20 at age 78, the Studio's profits soared from US$12.4 million to US$26.7 million (Bryman, 1995).

The Walt Disney Company

After Walt and Roy Disney passed away, their successors almost took the company down. The new leader Ronald Miller, Walt Disney's son-in-law, was unable to match the previous success. In 1983, the year Disney Channel began broadcasting and Tokyo Disneyland opened, Saul Steinberg, a New York financier, or a corporate raider in Disney's parlance, aggressively purchased Disney stock in an attempt to take over the company as he believed that the company had great assets but was poorly led. Then appeared Texas billionaires, Bass brothers, relatively friendly investors, who poured in nearly US$500 million and worked on finding new management to bring Disney back to the lucrative lane. In 1984, the year Disney established a new movie label Touchstone Pictures to sharpen its competitive edge to attract teenagers and adults, Bass hired former Paramount executive Michael Eisner and former Warner executive Frank Wells to run the Disney company. They then hired Jeffery Katzenberg, who had worked for Eisner at Paramount, to run Disney Studios. This shift from idea men to businessmen rejuvenated Disney for record profits under the management of "Team Disney," what this new management team was often called.

To honor the company founder, Eisner changed the company name to The Walt Disney Company in 1986. Mickey Mouse, a signifier of Disney, was the company logo. As Eisner put it,

> "Mickey... does not live in the temporal world of mortals. Instead, he and his Disney counterparts live in the hearts, memories, and minds of people everywhere. He is renewed with each generation...".
>
> (quoted in Wasko, 1996: 358)

Later, Eisner identified the corporate strategies as, first, to build the greatest entertainment asset base in the world, and second, to simultaneously create the greatest entertainment product in the world. He then launched new policies of reviving the traditional Disney, modernizing certain Disney characters, introducing diverse product lines, implementing severe cost-cutting, increasing prices at the theme parks dramatically, employing new technological developments, and promoting corporate synergy (Wasko, 2001).

In 1987, Disney's filmmaking hit new heights when the company for the first time became the leader of Hollywood studios in terms of box-office gross. *Good Morning, Vietnam* (1987), *Three Men and a Baby* (1987), *Who Framed Roger Rabbit* (1988), *Honey, I Shrunk the Kids* (1989), *Dick Tracy* (1990), *Pretty Woman* (1990), and *Sister Act* (1992), all passed the US$100 million milestone. Disney animated features also performed well with the best-selling *The Little Mermaid* (1989) being topped by *Beauty and the Beast* (1991), which was in turn topped by *Aladdin* (1992). In 1991, the company was one of the top 200 of all American corporations in terms of sales and assets, and ranked 43rd in terms of profits (Gomery, 1994). Two-thirds of the operation profits were contributed by the Parks division after heavy promotions and collaborations with filmmakers George Lucas and Francis Coppola to create new attractions in 1989, such as Star Tours, Splash Mountain, and the Disney–MGM Studios Theme Park, which was renamed Disney's Hollywood Studios in 2008. These attractions were mainly for teenagers because "Team Disney" was eager to change the company's image as just for kids for better revenue generation.

Disney marked unprecedented growth in the 1990s when the domestic and global economies were strong and the governments tended to deregulate for media and entertainment to prosper. From 1984 to 1994, Disney's annual profits quadrupled, and its stock price increased 1,300 percent (Iger, 2019). On April 12, 1992, Euro Disney, later renamed Disneyland Paris, opened. In 1994, Disney introduced its first Broadway stage production, *Beauty and the Beast*, followed by *The Lion King* in 1997, based on its 1994 blockbuster film. In 1995, Disney initiated the country's second largest corporate takeover to purchase Capital Cities/ABC Inc. for US$19 billion. In February 1996, Disney went online to launch its official website. In the same year, Radio Disney was launched. In 1998, a new theme park, Disney's Animal Kingdom, opened at Walt Disney World. By 1999, there were 725 Disney Stores around the world, up from 450 in 1996.

In 2001, the company honored the 100th anniversary of the birth of its founder, Walt Disney, with a celebration called "100 Years of Magic" centered at the Disney–MGM Studios in Florida. In this "magical" year, two new Disney theme parks opened: Disney's California Adventure, next to Anaheim Disneyland, in February, and Tokyo DisneySea, next to Tokyo Disneyland, in September. In March 2002, Walt Disney Studios adjacent to Disneyland Paris opened. In January 2003, ground was broken for Hong Kong Disneyland, which officially opened on September 12, 2005, the year Disneyland celebrated its 50th anniversary. In 2003, two Disney films, *Pirates of the Caribbean: The Curse of the Black Pearl* and *Finding Nemo*, grossed over US$300 million at the box office and made Disney the first studio in history to surpass US$3 billion at the global box office.

From year 2002, Eisner's leadership was publicly challenged by Walt's nephew, Roy Disney, who refused to retire from the board and later initiated the "Save Disney" campaign to oust Eisner for reasons such as the poor rating performances at ABC. Disney's internal uncertainty led to America's largest cable network Comcast's bid to acquire the company for US$64 billion. Although Comcast eventually withdrew its offer, disputes over the years clouded Eisner's two-decade Disney legacy. His role as chairman was discharged in the 2004 shareholder meeting, and he stepped down as Disney's chief executive officer in the end of September 2005, soon after the opening of Hong Kong Disneyland.

In October 2005, then chief operating officer Robert Iger succeeded Eisner as chief executive officer. As stated on the company's website, Iger's strategic vision focused on three fundamental aspects. First, generating the best creative content possible; second, fostering innovation and utilizing the latest technology; and third, expanding into new markets around the world. Iger started his career with ABC in 1974 and was chairman of the ABC Group in 1996 when "Team Disney" purchased the network. In 1999, he became president of Walt Disney International and was promoted to be Disney's chief operating officer in 2000. In 2012, Iger added an additional role as the company's chairman.

Through strategic alliances and acquisitions, Iger further transformed Disney. In his first board meeting as Disney's chief executive officer, Iger expressed his plan to acquire Pixar Animation Studios, an idea inspired by Hong Kong Disneyland's opening ceremony parade which featured many characters from the Pixar films Disney then distributed, but nothing from Disney's recent animated films (Iger, 2019). One year later in 2006, Disney successfully bought Pixar from Steve Jobs in a quickly proven rewarding US$7.4 billion deal, which was at first suspected to be too generous for a studio which produced one animated film a year. In 2009, Disney acquired Marvel Entertainment from Isaac Perlmutter for US$4 billion, which broadened Disney's appeals to boys and compensated its previous skew toward girls. In the same year, Disney reached an agreement to distribute live-action films made by DreamWorks, originally one of Disney's major competitors, for seven years under Disney's Touchstone Pictures banner. In October 2010, Disney signed a deal with China's Creative Power Entertaining Corporation to broadcast its top-rated animated series, *Pleasant Goat and Big Big Wolf*, on Disney Channels in 52 countries and regions. In 2012, Disney purchased LucasFilm from George Lucas for US$4 billion, adding the legendary *Star Wars* franchise to its empire. In 2019,

Disney closed a US$71 billion acquisition deal of Twenty-First Century Fox, Inc. with Rupert Murdoch.

Under Iger's leadership, Disney became one of the world's largest entertainment conglomerates with four main business segments: Media Networks; Disney Parks, Experiences and Products; Studio Entertainment; and Direct-to-Consumer and International, reorganized in 2018 from Media Networks, Parks and Resorts, Studio Entertainment, and Consumer Products and Interactive Media. On November 12, 2019, the company launched Disney Plus streaming service, which integrated Iger's strategic focuses on content, technology, and global reach. In one year, Disney Plus surpassed 73 million paid subscribers. Iger's contract as Disney's chief executive officer was renewed a few times to step down in year 2021. On February 25, 2020, Disney named Bob Chapek, head of Disney Parks, Experiences and Products, to succeed Iger as the company's chief executive officer, while Iger remained as executive chairman and directed Disney's creative endeavors through the end of his contract. In the succession announcement, Disney highlighted that, over the 15 years as CEO, Iger had increased the company's market capitalization fivefold. Chapek followed Iger's strategic visions, with the latest emphasis on the company's direct-to-consumer business.

"The Chinese Walt Disney Company"

As coined by Stanley Cheung, former managing director of The Walt Disney Company (China) Ltd., it is "The Chinese Walt Disney Company," not The Walt Disney Company in China to be operated. Such an announcement is not only to win the local market with stronger local relevance, but also to show Disney's promise to the Chinese party–state for better government relations. Compared to the other global cultural players, Disney has a relatively long history with more localization efforts in China.

Snow White and the Seven Dwarfs (1937) was the first Disney cultural content exposed in China, with its Asian premiere in Shanghai. This movie not only was an immediate commercial success, but also inspired Chinese film-making. In 1940, China made a live-action version of *Chinese Princess Snow White*. In 1941, China released the first Chinese animated feature film and the fourth animated feature film in the world, *Princess Iron Fan* (1941), adapted from the popular 16th-century Chinese mythological novel *Journey to the West*. In the Chinese market, localized Disney images of Mickey Mouse in a rickshaw, Minnie Mouse in Chinese cheongsam, Donald Duck on legendary Flaming Mountain, and Snow White with Chinese *baxianguohai* (Eight Immortals), were identified in the 1930s and 1940s (Mo, 2016). Disney appeared popular in China before the Chinese Communist Party took over mainland China from Kuomintang in 1949. Afterward, all capitalist products, including Disney's, were banned in the market.

In 1986, ten years after the Cultural Revolution ended, Disney's then chief executive officer Michael Eisner signed the first deal with China's national television station, China Central Television, to air 104 episodes of *Mickey Mouse and Donald Duck* on Sunday evenings for two years, starting in October 1986. This deal marked Disney's return to China. Two years later in 1988, Disney set up its regional headquarter in Hong Kong. In 1993, the Chinese government approved the publication of *Mickey Mouse Magazine*. In 1994, Disney's 30-minute daily television block *Dragon Club*, a renaming of *Mickey Mouse Club* to downplay the Disney flavor, premiered on September 19. Following the openness in late 1994, when China announced that ten foreign films per year would be released in the domestic market on a revenue-sharing basis, Disney's ice-breaking theatrical animated picture *The Lion King* was distributed in China in 1995. In 1996, Disney's live performances, *Disney on Ice*, started to tour around major cities. In 1997, Disney's VCD and DVD titles were formally released in China. In the same year, Disney announced that they would co-build Hong Kong Disneyland with the government of the Hong Kong Special Administrative Region. In August 2001, Disney Internet went online in China with the launch of its official website, Disney.com.cn.

Disney entered China for a substantial amount of time, but it was not until 2005 that the Mouse House appeared to be an active player in the Middle Kingdom. In order to understand the amount of Disney's news coverage in China over the years, I made an analysis via the *WiseNews* database, which showed a significant leap from 2004 to 2005: in the most popular market-oriented newspaper, *Southern Metropolis Daily*, Disney's reports increased from 164 to 380 and from 370 to 610 in Shanghai-based *Oriental Daily News*. Three milestone events took place in 2005 for Disney. First, on January 1, Hong Kongborn Stanley Cheung came on board as the managing director of The Walt Disney Company (China) Ltd. This appointment marked Disney's strategy to locally manage its businesses in China. Second, in August, Disney moved its regional headquarter to Shanghai from Hong Kong. This move signified Disney's official landing in mainland China. Third, on September 12, Hong Kong Disneyland opened.

Hong Kong Disneyland is the fifth Disneyland in the world and the third Disneyland outside of the United States, after 1983's Tokyo Disneyland and 1992's Euro Disneyland, later named Disneyland Paris.

As shown in China's National Enterprise Credit Information Publicity System, Disney registered The Walt Disney Company (Shanghai) Limited under Shanghai Municipal Administration of Industry and Commerce for 30 years on December 7, 2004. The company name was changed to The Walt Disney Company (China) Limited on July 17, 2015, with the business scope of investment management, capital operation and financial management, research development and technical support, employee training and management, marketing, intellectual property licensing and consultancy in the fields of consumer products and information industry (including trademarks and copyrights), and animation image design and production (excluding movie and television production).

Under Cheung's leadership, Disney's localization efforts intensified in all lines of business. Disney's local employees in China expanded from 70 to nearly 400 in 2005 and 600 in early 2010. In 2007, the first Chinese Walt Disney movie *The Secret of Magic Gourd*, based on a popular Chinese story, was released. This was the first Disney-branded movie made outside of Hollywood. In 2008, "The Chinese Walt Disney Company" pioneered its Princess campaign because the company believed that Princesses' selling power was underestimated under China's then one-child policy. The Princess campaign called for a synthesis across different business units. Unlike traditional projects that are imported from the United States, the Princess campaign was exported to the United States from China. To be in line with this Princess idea, the Sleeping Beauty Castle at Hong Kong Disneyland was re-translated to the Sleeping *Princess* Castle in Chinese.

Another project initiated by "The Chinese Walt Disney Company" was Disney English Learning Centers. In 2008, Disney launched its first English Learning Center in a central business district in Shanghai for children aged two to twelve. In just over one year after the launch of Disney English, seven English Language Learning Centers opened in Shanghai, with thousands of children enrolled in these programs. In 2010, Disney English Learning Centers were expanded from Shanghai to Beijing, as well as to other tier-one and tier-two cities across the nation, such as Chengdu (Sichuan province), Guangzhou (Guangdong province), Nanjing (Jiangsu province), and Shenzhen.

In July 2014, ten years into Cheung's tenure, Disney appointed a new managing director, Luke Kang, former managing director of

Disney Korea, to share practices across businesses and countries in Asia while China is growing to be Disney's biggest international market. In a talk to Beijing Chung Kong Graduate School of Business on June 15, 2015, titled "Finding Our Place in China's Entertainment Industry—with Greater China of Disney," Kang summarized his three core strategies as locally appealing content, digital connections, and consumer engagement. One example he mentioned in the talk was the establishment of the Local Content team in 2012 to "create content in local for local." For example, the animated series *Stoney and Rocky*. This series featured two young Chinese stone lions' adventures in China around traditional Chinese themes such as Peking opera and Autumn Festival mooncakes, as *People's Daily*, newspaper of the Chinese Communist Party, reported.

Hong Kong Disneyland and Shanghai Disneyland

Although Hong Kong Disneyland and Shanghai Disneyland are located in China, they do not report to The Walt Disney Company (China) Ltd., but directly report to the United States as part of the Parks division.

Hong Kong Disneyland

Cultural industries are concerned in part with the representation of the culture and history of a place (Urry, 1995). Before examining Hong Kong Disneyland, I will first review Hong Kong's encounters with the West, which brought certain proximity for Hong Kong to be the first Disneyland city in China.

Hong Kong was largely created by Western colonialism in the aftermath of the Opium Wars. Hong Kong Island was officially acquired by the British Empire under the Treaty of Nanjing in 1842. It was the first so-called unequal treaty in China due to the 1939–1942 Opium War. In 1860, Britain further acquired Hong Kong Kowloon and Stonecutters Island under the Treaty of Beijing after the second Opium War. In 1898, the Convention for the Extension of Hong Kong Territory granted the British the right to lease Hong Kong New Territories for 99 years until June 30, 1997. This convention confirmed Britain's full governance over the whole Hong Kong territory.

In 1984, China and Britain reached an agreement on Hong Kong. Based on this Sino–British Joint Declaration, the British agreed to return the New Territories they leased, as well as Hong Kong Island and Kowloon acquired by the Opium Wars, for both political and moral reasons (Morris, 1997). China, on the other hand, agreed to retain Hong Kong's social and economic systems, as well as its lifestyle, for a further 50 years until 2047 under the "basic law" based on then Chinese President Deng Xiaoping's principle of "one country, two systems" to maintain prosperity and stability in Hong Kong. In other words, the basic law serves as the formal constitutional document that guarantees systematic continuity in Hong Kong of capitalist economies, the enjoyment of autonomy, and the practice of governance characterized by Hong Kong people ruling Hong Kong (Hook, 2000). China regained Hong Kong on July 1, 1997, when the last British governor of Hong Kong, Chris Patten, handed Hong Kong back to China. Over the 150 years of British governance, excluding a period of Japanese occupation from 1941 to 1945, Hong Kong has undoubtedly become the most Westernized city in China.

Disney and the Hong Kong government reached an agreement in 1999 to build Hong Kong Disneyland, a pilot or a dress rehearsal for Shanghai Disneyland (Matusitz, 2011). With the shortest construction time of Disneyland yet, Hong Kong Disneyland, the fifth Disneyland in the world, opened to the public on September 12, 2005 for "wholesome family entertainment" (Slater, 1999).

Located on a landfill of Penny Bay on Hong Kong's largest outlying island Lantau Island, Hong Kong Disneyland is owned by a joint venture company, the Hong Kong International Theme Parks Limited, with two shareholders: The Walt Disney Company and the Government of the Hong Kong Special Administration Region (HKSRG). An agreement between these two parties was signed on December 10, 1999. The construction on Hong Kong Disneyland began with a groundbreaking ceremony on January 12, 2003. HKSRG approached Disney for Hong Kong Disneyland to establish Hong Kong as "Asia's World City," not just China's special administration region (Lo, 2005). Due to financial loss at Disneyland Paris, Disney minimized its risk at Hong Kong Disneyland through fewer money investments and a smaller physical size of the park. For the initial construction, HKSRG owned 57 percent and Disney 43 percent of Hong Kong Disneyland. After the later expansion projects invested by Disney, HKSRG's ownership shifted to 53 percent, and Disney to 47 percent in the end of 2016, when eight themed lands and areas were built: Adventureland, Fantasyland, Grizzly Gulch, Main Street USA, Marvel's Iron Man, Mystic Point, Tomorrowland, and Toy Story Land.

The opening of Hong Kong Disneyland was regarded as a big triumph for Disney. Disney rejected the Hong Kong government's idea to broadly reflect Chinese culture by arguing the importance of a genuine

Disney experience, a formula proven successful at Tokyo Disneyland. Consequently, Hong Kong Disneyland bears all the hallmarks of the Anaheim original. However, icons reminding people of strong American nationalism were cautiously removed, and local cuisines and snacks, such as dim-sum and fish balls, were served. Language is another aspect of localization that better engages the local audience. Signs at Hong Kong Disneyland are written in both English and traditional Chinese and the employees are equipped with English, Cantonese, and Mandarin.

Another surface localization effort is the incorporation of Chinese Feng Shui into the design of Hong Kong Disneyland to maximize energy and guest flow. For example, water plays an important role in good Chinese Feng Shui. As a result, lakes, ponds, and streams, as well as a big fountain, are placed at Hong Kong Disneyland to invite good fortune. Another example of Feng Shui is the use of Chinese prosperous numbers, such as 2,238 and 888. Decorating the Chinese restaurant at the Hong Kong Disneyland Hotel are 2,238 crystal lotuses, because the number sounds like the phrase "easily generates wealth" in Cantonese. The main ballroom at the Disneyland Hotel is 888 square meters because 888 is considered a number that brings triple wealth.

Shanghai Disneyland

When being asked why Shanghai was chosen to build Disneyland, Robert Iger, former chief executive officer of The Walt Disney Company said, "Shanghai is the most dynamic city in China" (Levine, 2016). Before reviewing the making of Shanghai Disneyland, I will first examine Shanghai's encounters with the West and the city's openness to foreign cultures that made Shanghai the second Disneyland city in China. After the country's reform and economic opening up in late 1970s, Shanghai was deemed as the cosmopolitan representative city of China and China's gateway to Western modernity (Bergère, 2009).

In 1842, the Treaty of Nanjing opened Shanghai as one of the five Chinese ports for British trade. By 1853, Shanghai had surpassed Guangzhou as China's premiere trading city (Wu, 1999). In 1844, the Treaty of Huangpu granted the same privileges to France as the Treaty of Nanjing had to Britain. That is, the same five ports were open to French merchants and citizens who enjoyed extraterritorial privileges in town. Also, France was approved for a fixed tariff on Sino–French trade and the right to station consuls.

Through the trade with the West, the treaty ports enjoyed a commercial and industrial boom. Among them, Shanghai, rather than Guangzhou, Fuzhou, Xiamen, or Ningbo, is the most West friendly and modernized because of its business tradition of openness to outsiders. Shanghai had been a market town of the Yangtze Delta since the 15th century as an export city for nearby cotton-rich provinces in exchange for rice and tea from central and southern provinces. Trade continued to expand throughout the 18th century, and Shanghai became a network of transportation. Its commercial rise led to a greater demand for money and banking, which further solidified Shanghai as China's mercantile center and gateway to Western modernity. By 1930, Shanghai became the fifth largest city in the world and was identified as "the Paris of Asia" (Lee, 1999), with the most highly developed urban amenities (next to Tokyo) built by the foreign officials in Asia.

After the Chinese Communist Party took over China in 1949, Shanghai experienced more than 30 years of disinvestment, while contributed about 25 percent of the country's revenues during the 1970s (Hao & Lin, 1994). Shanghai re-opened up to the world in the late 19th century when modern industrial development commenced in Shanghai. In 1986, the Chinese State Council issued a written approval of Shanghai's comprehensive plan, stating that "after several decades of hard work, Shanghai should be built into a socialist modern metropolis with prosperous economy" (Zhang, 2014). Since then, Shanghai has been an ambitious site of reform.

In 1990, based on the model of China's Special Economic Zones, the Pudong New Area to the east of Shanghai and Huangpu River was established, the Shanghai Stock Exchange was opened, and the Lujiazui Finance and Trade Zone was approved as the first of its kind in China. Planned as a three-phase development, Pudong is larger than the central city to relieve the spatial pressure on old central Shanghai, which largely represents a historical legacy from the European concessions prior to 1949. Pudong also serves as a new center for industrial and commercial activities to regain Shanghai's pre-1949 position as the leading industrial and trading center in China and East Asia. The Lujiazui Central Business District's ambition to rebuild the Bund, which housed over 100 financial buildings before 1949 as China's Wall Street, is an example of Shanghai's return to its international position.

In 1992, the 14th Chinese Communist Party Central Committee appointed Shanghai to serve as the "dragon head" of economic growth in the whole Yangtze basin, as well as an international economic, financial, and trade center. The 2010 Shanghai Expo accelerated the city's international outlook. In 2013, the State Council approved the establishment of the Shanghai Pilot Free Trade Zone in Pudong, the first Hong Kong-like free trade area in Mainland China, which further promoted Shanghai's status as the country's international representative.

The negotiation for Shanghai Disney Resort was a decade long, having started in 1999. China's former Premiere Zhu Rongji, who was mayor of Shanghai from 1987 to 1991, was the one who first joined the conversation of building Disneyland in Shanghai. The Shanghai Disney Resort project in the Pudong district was finally approved by the Chinese government in November 2009, two weeks before then President of the United States Barack Obama's visit to China.

Shanghai Disneyland is a joint venture between The Walt Disney Company and the state-owned Shanghai Shendi Group. It has two owner companies, Shanghai International Theme Park Company Limited and Shanghai International Theme Park Associated Facilities Company Limited, and one management company, Shanghai International Theme Park and Resort Management Company Limited. The management company is responsible for designing and operating the resort on behalf of the owner companies. In the owner companies, Shanghai Shendi Group holds 57 percent of the shares and Disney holds the remaining 43 percent of shares. In the joint venture management company, which is entitled to receive management fees based on the operating performance of the resort, Disney has a 70 percent stake, and Shanghai Shendi Group has a 30 percent stake. Shanghai Disneyland and Resort, Disney's largest foreign investment to date with a reported first-stage investment of US$3.7 billion, later amended to US$5.5 billion, is Disney's fourth theme park outside of the United States.

Disney appointed Philippe Gas, former head of Disneyland Paris since 2008, as general manager of Shanghai Disneyland, effective from September 2014. Gas joined Disney in 1991. With an understanding that China was very different from his home country of France, he saw the Chinese government "as a guide, as an advisor" that helped to create better products. To Gas, Shanghai Disneyland, which he was engaged to build, had a simple goal to "allow family or friends to spend a moment together in an environment that allows them to get away from their day-to-day life, and create a memory that will last with them" (Nunlist, 2016). The Chinese government was reported to have supervised everything from the price of admission to the types of rides at Shanghai Disneyland.

While Gas took care of the operation, Disney's then chief executive officer Robert Iger was the guiding force of Shanghai Disneyland by initiating the creative direction of being "authentically Disney and distinctly Chinese." China was an important market that greatly demanded Iger's attention. He has stated, "We need China to be stable and continue to create growth in order to create growth in our company"

(Frater, 2014). In order to profit from the lucrative Chinese market, Iger was reported to have attended to every detail of the park design, such as proposing moss on the stones of the castle to make the castle look old, pre-tasting more than 200 dishes on restaurant menus, trying every ride before the park opening, and finalizing all shows, including the characters appearing in the daily parade.

Efforts made were not one-sided. Being the majority shareholder of Shanghai Disneyland, Disney's Chinese partner was also eager to boost the park's success. The authorities cleared a 1,700-acre area, relocated residents, moved graves, and closed more than 150 polluting factories for the construction of the resort. Infrastructure was also enhanced by a new subway to the park. In addition, protection of Disney's intellectual properties from piracy has intensified, such as fining copycat Disney hotels near Shanghai Disneyland and seizing thousands of counterfeit Disney items in Hangzhou, a city near Shanghai.

Piracy is a major challenge for Disney's business in China. To pave the way for the opening of Shanghai Disneyland, China's State Administration for Industry and Commerce of China (SAIC) published a notice on October 19, 2015, announcing a one-year campaign through October 2016 that aimed to protect the trademarks of The Walt Disney Company and crack down on related piracy in China, especially near Shanghai Disneyland. It is rare for the Chinese government to launch a special campaign targeting the counterfeiting of a particular brand. According to an SAIC notice, this campaign was to protect consumers' interests, promote fair competition in the market, and enhance the country's image.

The Shanghai Disneyland opening ceremony was held at noon on June 16, 2016. Then Shanghai Mayor Yang Xiong stressed that the combination of "classic Disney and brilliant Chinese style at Shanghai Disneyland" would help Shanghai become a global tourist city. Disney's then chief executive officer Robert Iger read Shanghai Disneyland's dedication, a tradition started by Walt Disney himself: "... Shanghai Disneyland is your land... Shanghai Disneyland is authentically Disney and distinctly Chinese..." It was the first time the localized "distinctly Chinese" creative direction was engraved in a Disneyland dedication. Iger considered Shanghai Disneyland opening as "one of the proudest and most exciting moments in the Company's history" (Shanghai Daily, 2016). In the opening ceremony speech, he described Shanghai Disneyland as "a celebration of creativity and collaboration, commitment and patience, the triumph of imagination and innovation, and a testament to the strong partnership between Disney and China."

In addition, Iger read a congratulatory letter from then President of the United States Barack Obama stating that Shanghai Disneyland blended "American business with the beauty and rich cultural heritage of China" and "captured the promise of the bilateral relationship between the U.S. and China." In return, Wang Yang, then Chinese vice-premier, shared a letter from Chinese President Xi Jinping, who congratulated the successful cooperation between Shanghai and The Walt Disney Company...

> "By adding to the classic Disney style a stroke of Chinese characteristics, and by blending international standards with best local practices, the resort demonstrates our commitment to cross-cultural cooperation and our innovation mentality in the new era."

Overall, Xi regarded Shanghai Disneyland as a symbol that demonstrated China's openness and good will to boost the Sino–US relationship.

Shanghai Disneyland's opening during a rain shower did not bother the Chinese party–state representative Wang Yang. After reading Xi's letter, Wang said that the rain was a sign of fortune for being the "rain of U.S. dollars and Chinese renminbi." This "rain of wealth" brought Shanghai Disneyland's entrance admissions, a major source of the park's revenues, into examination. Shanghai Disneyland tickets went on sale on March 28, 2016. A single-day adult ticket cost about US$75 (RMB 499) during the grand-opening period (June 16 to Jun 30, 2016), weekends, designated holidays, and summer holidays (July and August), and about US$55 (RMB 370) on non-peak days. Children (1.4 meters and below), seniors (65 years old and above), and guests with disabilities received discounts of 25 percent, and infants (one meter and below) got free admission. A two-day ticket had a 5 percent discount.

Such ticket pricing, "based on in-depth market research and analysis conducted with a wide range of Chinese consumers, industry experts, and local regulators," according to the Shanghai Disneyland website, was claimed to be "reasonable" when compared with US$125 and US$105 at Disney World in Florida. Chinese media also defended Disney over its ticket prices because pricing was co-decided by Disney and its Chinese partner. "It (Disneyland) is a premium brand... and they can set the price and let the market decide," commented *China Youth Daily*, newspaper of the Chinese Communist Youth League. However, the "premium" yet "reasonable" entrance admissions of Shanghai Disneyland were in fact substantial to the local Chinese. According to the National Bureau of Statistics of China, in 2016, the average monthly disposable income in China per person was about

US$298 (annually RMB 23,821) and about US$420 in cities (annually RMB 33,616). Not to mention that the consumption of tourist services is mostly social which normally involves a particular social grouping. In the case of Shanghai Disneyland, taking into account every multigenerational visit contributed by a family of three (parents and one child) or of five or of seven (including grandparents), it is not surprising that the Chinese official saw the opening rain as dollar signs.

Shanghai Disneyland and Hong Kong Disneyland: Complements or competitors?

In response to the construction of Shanghai Disneyland, Andrew Kam, former managing director of Hong Kong Disneyland, commented on Hong Kong Disneyland's webpage in April 2011, that "we look forward to growing together with Shanghai and capturing the significant growth of the Asian leisure travel market in the years to come." Stanley Cheung, former managing director of The Walt Disney Company (China) Ltd. and a board member of Shanghai Disneyland, also emphasized in his August 2014 talk at The Chinese University of Hong Kong that Shanghai Disneyland and Hong Kong Disneyland were complements to each other, not competitors because the Chinese market was big enough. According to the National Bureau of Statistics of China, in 2015, domestic travel in China reached 4 billion visits and overseas travel reached nearly 128 million visits. Moreover, research showed that people who liked Disney tended to visit all Disneyland not just one, Cheung stressed. When Shanghai Disneyland opened, Hong Kong Disneyland became one of the top search queries online. That is, the opening of Shanghai Disneyland, to some extent, brought Hong Kong Disneyland under the spotlight and promoted the park.

Disney believes that the world's most populous country China, with 1.4 billion people, has room for two Disneyland in Hong Kong and Shanghai, as in the United States with the population of 350 million, there are two thriving Disney parks in California and Florida. Samuel Lau, former managing director of Hong Kong Disneyland, stressed the different sources of Hong Kong Disneyland's visitors: "Shanghai Disneyland offers the mainland Chinese visitors an opportunity to experience and learn more about Disneyland... For Hong Kong Disneyland, visitors are mainly from Southern China, Southeast Asia and Hong Kong" (Ren, 2016). According to Hong Kong Disneyland's annual financial reports, from 2010 to 2015, the majority of the park's visitors were from mainland China. In fiscal year 2016, there was a 5 percent increase in international visitors and 5 percent decrease in mainland Chinese visitors while the percentage of local Hong Kong visitors remained the same.

To be consistent with the company's narrative of complementing with, not competing with Shanghai Disneyland, Hong Kong Disneyland has been eager to increase its international outlook through promotional campaigns. For example, in 2015, Hong Kong Disneyland worked with *MasterChef Asia*, which broadcasted in Southeast Asia, Hong Kong, Taiwan, and Macau, to host the program's contestants. In return, the program dedicated one full episode to Hong Kong Disneyland in celebration of the park's 10th anniversary. "International" appears to be the keyword for Hong Kong Disneyland. While the city of Hong Kong promotes its status as "Asia's World City," Hong Kong Disneyland is positioning itself as Southeast Asia's Disneyland to avoid competing with Shanghai Disneyland, China's Disneyland.

Bibliography

Bergère, M. (2009). *Shanghai: China's gateway to modernity*. Stanford, CA: Stanford University Press.

Bryman, A. (1995). *Disney and his worlds*. New York: Routledge.

Davis, S. (1996). The theme park: global industry and cultural form. *Media, Culture & Society*, *18*, 399–422.

Frater, P. (2014, August 1). France's Philippe gas to head Shanghai Disneyland. *Variety*. Retrieved February 1, 2020, from http://variety.com/2014/biz/asia/frances-philippe-gas-to-head-shanghai-disneyland-1201273528/.

Gitlin, T. (2001). *Media unlimited: How the torrent of images and sounds overwhelms our lives*. New York: Henry Holt and Company.

Gomery, D. (1994). Disney's business history: A reinterpretation. In Smoodin, E. (Ed.), *Disney discourse: Producing the Magic Kingdom*, 71–86. New York: Routledge.

Gottdiner, M. (1982). Disneyland: A utopian urban space. *Journal of Contemporary Ethnohraphy*, 11, 139–162.

Hao, J. & Lin, Z. (1994). *Changing central-local relations in China: Reform and state capacity*. New York: Westview Press.

Harrington, S. (2015). *The Disney Fetish*. Bloomington, IN: Indiana University Press.

Hook, B. (2000). Hong Kong under Chinese sovereignty: A preliminary assessment. In Ash, R. et al. (Ed.), *Hong Kong in transition: The handover years*, 95–112. London: Macmillan.

Iger, R. (2019). *The ride of a lifetime: Lessons learned from 15 years as CEO of the Walt Disney Company*. New York: Random House.

Lee, L. (1999). Shanghai modern: Reflections on urban culture in China in the 1930s. *Public Culture*, 11(1), 75–107.

Lee, N. & Madej, K. (2012). *Disney stories: Getting to digital*. New York: Springer.
Levine, A. (2016, June 23). Bob Iger: Shanghai Disney isn't just Disneyland in China. *USA Today*. Retrieved December 10, 2019, from http://www.usatoday.com/story/travel/experience/america/2016/06/23/bob-iger-interview-shanghai-disney-resort-opening/86253624/.
Lo, K.C. (2005). *Chinese face/off: The transnational popular culture of Hong Kong*. Champaign: University of Illinois Press.
Matusitz, J. (2011). Disney's successful adaptation in Hong Kong: A glocalization perspective. *Asia Pacific Journal of Management*, 28(4), 667–668.
Mo, T. (2016). What changes will Shanghai Disney make? (in Chinese). *Xinmin Weekly*, 24, 16–23.
Morris, J. (1997). *Hong Kong*. New York: Random House.
Nunlist, T. (2016, December 15). Behind the scenes in the Magic Kingdom. *CKGSB Knowledge*. Retrieved January 5, 2020, from https://knowledge.ckgsb.edu.cn/2016/12/15/conversations/shanghai-disney-resort-behind-scenes/.
Ren, H.L. (2016, June 16). Disney's overflow and shift out (in Chinese). *Xinmin Weekly*, 24, 24–27.
Shanghai Daily (2016, July 13). Disney chief claims a million people visited park. *Shanghai Daily*. Retrieved January, 5, 2020, from https://www.sohu.com/a/104993670_161402.
Slater, J. (1999). Aieeyaaa! A mouse. *Far East Economic Review*, 162(45), 50–51.
Smith, A.D. (1995). *Nations and nationalism in a global era*. Oxford: Polity.
Smith, D. (2001). *The quotable Walt Disney*. New York: Disney Editions.
Urry, J. (1995). *Consuming places*. London: Routledge.
Wallace, M. (1985). Mickey Mouse history: Portraying the past at Disney World. *Radical History Review*, 32, 33–57.
Wasko, J. (1996). Understanding the Disney Universe. In Curran, J. & Gurevitch, M. (Ed.), *Mass media and society*, 348–365. New York: Arnold.
Wasko, J. (2001). *Understanding Disney: The manufacture of fantasy*. Cambridge: Polity.
Watts, S. (2001). *The magic kingdom: Walt Disney and the American way of life*. Columbia, MO: University of Missouri Press.
Wu, W. (1999). City profile Shanghai. *Cities*, 16(3), 207–216.
Yu, H. (2014). From Kundun to Mulan: A political economic case study of Disney and China. *Asia Network Exchange*, 22(1), 13–22.
Zhang, L.Y. (2014). Dynamics and constraints of State-led global city formation in emerging economies: The case of Shanghai. *Urban Studies*, 51(6), 1162–1178.

3 Ownership structure of Shanghai Disneyland

Shanghai Disneyland is a joint venture between The Walt Disney Company and the state-owned Shanghai Shendi Group (Shendi), which was established in August 2010. Shendi's chairman, Fan Xiping, was the vice-secretary general of the Shanghai municipal government. This joint venture is comprised of two owner companies and one management company. All three companies were registered on April 2, 2011, according to China's National Enterprise Credit Information Publicity System. The management company is responsible for designing and operating the resort on behalf of the owner companies. In the owner companies, Shendi holds 57 percent of the shares, and Disney holds the remaining 43 percent of shares. In the joint venture management company, Disney has a 70 percent stake and Shendi holds 30 percent of Shanghai Disneyland (Table 3.1). For the management of Shanghai Disneyland in the joint venture management company, Disney is entitled to receive management fees based on operating performance of the resort. Shanghai Disney Resort, with a reported first-stage investment of US$3.7 billion, later amended to US$5.5 billion, is Disney's largest foreign investment so far.

Shanghai Disneyland has a different ownership structure from the other Disneyland. Before further examining the ownership structure of Shanghai Disneyland, I will first attend to Disney's ownership in the other Disneyland outside of the United States: Tokyo Disneyland, Disneyland Paris, and Hong Kong Disneyland, to understand the differences of Shanghai Disneyland.

Table 3.1 Ownership structure of Shanghai Disneyland

	Disney	*Shanghai Shendi Group*
Owner companies	43%	57%
Management company	70%	30%

Disney's ownership in overseas Disneyland: Tokyo, Paris, Hong Kong, and Shanghai

Tokyo Disneyland

Opened in 1983, Tokyo Disneyland was the first Disneyland built outside of the United States. It is a special case in terms of its ownership. Instead of investing in Tokyo Disneyland, Disney licensed Tokyo Disneyland to a local Japanese company, Oriental Land Co., Ltd., with zero percent of ownership but earnings of royalties on revenues. The main reason that accounted for Disney's authorization of Oriental Land Co., Ltd. to fully own and operate Tokyo Disneyland was financial concerns. During a time of financial predicament as discussed in the histories of the company, Disney was conservative about the risk of investing in the new business of international Disneyland. To Disney's surprise, Tokyo Disneyland enjoyed great business success right from its opening. Its phenomenal success boosted Disney's ambition and confidence in building another Disneyland outside of the United States.

Disneyland Paris

After considering more than 200 possible sites, Marne-la-Vallée, about 20 miles east of Paris, was chosen to host Euro Disneyland, which opened in 1992 (Matusitz, 2010). The name of Euro Disney was changed to Disneyland Paris in 1994. According to Disney's annual financial report, Disney owned 81 percent of Disneyland Paris at the end of fiscal year 2015, up from 49 percent in 1992. Unlike the arrangement with Shanghai Disneyland, there is no joint-venture management company for Disneyland Paris; it is 100 percent managed by Disney. The revenue performance of Disneyland Paris was disappointing. During its 14 years of business before Shanghai Disneyland opened in 2016, the park was reported to have only made profits for two years with a maximum loss of US$400 million. Euro Disney S.C.A, the owner company of Disneyland Paris, had been bailed out three times in three decades. The execution of Disneyland Paris was deemed as problematic, with issues, such as cultural missteps without considering local preferences and overstaffing from the very beginning. While making efforts to improve the management of Disneyland Paris, Disney continued its global expansion of another international Disneyland to enhance overall revenue performance for its parks business.

Hong Kong Disneyland

Opened in 2005, Hong Kong Disneyland is owned by a joint venture company, the Hong Kong International Theme Parks Limited, with two shareholders: The Walt Disney Company and the Government of the Hong Kong Special Administration Region (HKSRG). For the initial construction, HKSRG covered 90 percent of the US$1.8 billion cost but owned 57 percent of Hong Kong Disneyland. The closed-door Hong Kong Disneyland deal was called an unequal treaty by a local legislator (Choi, 2010). The Hong Kong government leased the land for free. Taking into account the infrastructure cost, such as highways and a 3.5-kilometer new railroad, HKSRG in total invested US$2.9 billion with an estimation that it would create 30,000 jobs (Lee & Fung, 2013). As former chief secretary of HKSRG Anson Chan emphasized, Disney and Hong Kong were both internationally well-known brand names and one could not put a price on Disney's choosing Hong Kong as a partner (Lee, 2009). After the later expansion projects invested in by Disney, HKSRG's ownership shifted to 53 percent and Disney's to 47 percent at the end of the fiscal year 2016. Unlike the arrangement for Shanghai Disneyland, there is no joint-venture management company for Hong Kong Disneyland; it is 100 percent managed by Disney.

According to Hong Kong Disneyland's annual financial reports, since its opening in 2005 until fiscal year 2019, only three years, fiscal years 2012 to 2014, showed net profits. In September 2020, due to economic concerns, the Hong Kong government ended Disney's land expansion option. As a pilot park for Disney's business in China, the underperformance of Hong Kong Disneyland did not stop Disney from investing in populous mainland China to attract more Chinese tourists to a nearby location.

Shanghai Disneyland

Except for the special pilot case of Tokyo Disneyland, Disney holds less ownership in Shanghai Disneyland than in all Disneyland outside of the United States (Table 3.2). Although Disney also holds the minority in Hong Kong Disneyland, the investments in Hong Kong Disneyland and Shanghai Disneyland are different due to different contexts. In the case of Hong Kong Disneyland, Disney's Hong Kong partner poured in a larger amount of investment because the city was eager to obtain a World City status through partnering with Disneyland. On the contrary, in the case of Shanghai Disneyland, Disney was keen

Table 3.2 Disney's ownership in Disneyland outside of the United States*

Park	Opening date	Disney's ownership
Tokyo Disneyland, Japan	April 15, 1983	0%*
Disneyland Paris, France	April 12, 1992	81%
Hong Kong Disneyland, China	September 12, 2005	47%
Shanghai Disneyland, China	June 16, 2016	43%

* Licensed to a local company with earnings of royalties on revenues.

on building Disneyland in China to create brand awareness and affinity for all lines of business in the world's second largest economy.

China has strict foreign investment policy. *The Catalogue for the Guidance of Foreign Investment Industries*, co-published by the Chinese National Development and Reform Commission, which governs China's economic development, and the Ministry of Commerce, which guides China's trade and investment policy, regulates the scope of foreign investment in different sectors of the economy in China. Overall, the *Catalogue* indicated four categories of foreign investment: the encouraged, the restricted, the prohibited, and the permitted (for industries that are not included in the *Catalogue*). Industries in the encouraged category enjoyed simplified approval procedures and favorable tax treatment, while restricted industries were subject to more approval requirements and a higher level of government scrutiny.

The construction of theme parks was one of the restricted investments, which were required to follow the Sino–foreign joint venture only rule and the majority Chinese ownership rule. The joint venture only rule required a foreign investor to find a Chinese partner in order to create a joint venture, and the majority Chinese ownership rule allowed foreign investors to hold less than 50 percent shares. Following the government requirements, Shanghai Disneyland was a joint venture between The Walt Disney Company and the state-owned Shanghai Shendi Group with two owner companies: Shanghai International Theme Park Company Limited and Shanghai International Theme Park Associated Facilities Company Limited. In the owner companies, Shanghai Shendi Group holds 57 percent of the shares and Disney holds the remaining 43 percent. Shanghai Disneyland is the first case in which Disney poured in a full cash investment without partial investment offset by its intellectual properties.

When the park opened, six out of the twelve board members in the owner companies of Shanghai Disneyland were from Shanghai Shendi Group: Fan Xiping was vice-secretary general of the Shanghai municipal government, Ma Yonghua was secretary general of the Shanghai State-Owned Assets Supervision and Management Commission, Shao Xiaoyun was Chinese Communist Party (CCP) deputy secretary of The Shanghai Airlines Corporation Limited, while Wang Qingguo, Cheng Fang, and Qiu Yichuan were members of the CCP but did not specify any titles associated with the government or the state-owned enterprises. As the majority ownership holder of Shanghai Disneyland, Shanghai Shendi Group demanded to be in full charge of three key aspects: construction time, cost control, and localization. As Fan Xiping, chairman of Shanghai Shendi Group, stated,

> "Disney is like driving a car in an unfamiliar country. Shendi is the local guide for driver Disney to go in the right direction… The bottom line is to follow China's regulations without jeopardizing China's core interests, including economic, cultural and social interests."
>
> (Ren, 2016)

Disney's minority ownership in Shanghai Disneyland due to Chinese national policy of protectionism in a way protects Disney by minimizing the geopolitical risk. In China, the party–state is entitled to suspend any media service at any time by direct order. Sometimes media bans go beyond cultural protectionism for political reasons. For example, in response to the South Korea government's decision in July 2016 to install the United States-made Terminal High Altitude Area Defense missiles, whose missile system's radar can not only defend against North Korea but also be used to spy into China, China's State Administration of Press, Publication, Radio, Film and Television banned the exposure of Korean content, formats, and artists in China, as well as Chinese–Korean co-production with a direct order.

The political relationship between the global capital's home country and the host country China is crucial for global cultural companies. In early 2017, Disney expressed the company's concerns about then President of the United States Donald Trump's threatening to levy tariffs of up to 45 percent on goods imported from China. Robert Iger, then chief executive officer of The Walt Disney Company, stated, "an all-out trade war with China would be damaging to Disney's business and to business in general" (Solomon, 2017). Disney might be less worried about Shanghai Disneyland because its Chinese partner holds the majority of ownership. However, for the other lines of business, such as movie imports and consumer products, Disney's business performance is at risk if the China–USA relationship turns negative and Disney fails to conciliate the Chinese government.

In addition to the two owner companies, Shanghai Disneyland has one management company, Shanghai International Theme Park and

Resort Management Company Limited, which is responsible for designing and operating the resort on behalf of the owner companies. In this joint venture, Disney has a 70 percent stake and Shanghai Shendi Group has a 30 percent interest. Holding 30 percent of the interests, Shanghai Shendi Group is entitled to appoint senior executives. Three out of the ten board members in the management company of Shanghai Disneyland when it opened were from Shanghai Shendi Group. Disney owned the majority of the management company because, unlike the construction of theme parks, which was one of the restricted businesses, management of entertainment venues fell under the encouraged category in China's *Catalogue for the Guidance of Foreign Investment Industries* with no obligation to follow the majority Chinese ownership rule.

Although theme park management belonged to the encouraged category, Disney did not own 100 percent but 70 percent of the management company of Shanghai Disneyland. For Disney, this is an exclusive arrangement. In the cases of Disneyland Paris and Hong Kong Disneyland, Disney takes 100 percent charge of the management. Such an arrangement for Shanghai Disneyland is not only to practically learn what the local audience expects for better revenue generation, but also to strategically show the company's respect for its local partners, as Disney's former chief executive officer Robert Iger often emphasized, for better government relations.

Shanghai Disneyland appeared to have arrived at the perfect time. First, openness to global forces was a political agenda in China. The Chinese government welcomed global companies to share both their economic capital of money wealth and cultural capital of symbolically powerful attributes when local industries were developing themselves. At the Davos 2017, contrary to then president of the United States Donald Trump's protectionism, Chinese President Xi Jinping emphasized the importance of embracing globalization as it is "impossible to swim away from the ocean of globalization" and "pursuing protectionism is like locking oneself in a dark room." Such statements echoed Xi's congratulatory letter for the opening of Shanghai Disneyland: "The resort demonstrates our commitment to cross-cultural cooperation and our innovation mentality in the new era."

Under such an agenda, the Chinese government welcomed foreign investment in promoting tourism, especially when the economic growth was slowing. In early November 2015, the government lowered its official five-year annual GDP growth target to 6.5 percent, the slowest pace since the 2008–2009 global financial crisis. Shanghai Disneyland was estimated to bring 10 to 15 million tourists to Shanghai every year. Other foreign capitals, such as Comcast NBC Universal, also entered China's tourism market. Universal Studios Beijing, approved by China's National Development and Reform Commission in September 2014 and broke ground in October 2016, was scheduled to open in 2021, under a deal signed in 2015 by Comcast NBC Universal and the state-owned Beijing Shouhuan Cultural Tourism Investment Co. Ltd. This project was reported to cost US$8 billion, including the expansion of a subway line to the park site in the Tongzhou district, east to Beijing. Universal Studios Beijing will be the sixth Universal Studios in the world, the third in Asia, and the biggest Universal Studios ever built.

Second, the Chinese middle-class's longing for family entertainment was on the rise, and the common family was expanding under the two-child policy effective from January 1, 2016. The emerging-middle class (households with annual disposable income of US$10,001 to $16,000), middle class (US$16,001 to $24,000), upper-middle-class households (US$24,001 to $46,000), and affluent households (more than US$46,000) were all on the rise. The middle-class, especially upper-middle-class and affluent households, greatly drove the consumption economy. The rising middle-class was believed to expect quality entertainment, which Disney had a good reputation for.

Third, Disneyland had a strong competitive edge, as local competitors were still developing their expertise. On May 28, 2016, about 20 days before the Shanghai Disneyland opening, the 494-acre Wanda Cultural Tourism City Nanchang, often called Nanchang Wanda City, opened in an attempt to fend off the Western import of Disneyland. Nanchang, capital of Jiangxi province, is about 450 miles away from Shanghai. Nanchang Wanda City was a US$3.2 billion project, aiming for 10 million visitors annually. Dalian Wanda Group's billionaire chairman, Wang Jianlin, who declared a patriotic war on Disney on China Central Television on May 22, 2016, claimed that 15 Wanda Cities in China would be "a pack of wolves" taking down the "only tiger," Shanghai Disneyland, by year 2020. However, due to financial losses, Wanda stepped back from competing with Disney one year later by largely selling its stake in tourist attractions.

To rival Disney, Wanda was keen on hiring former Disney executives. In October 2016, Andrew Kam, former managing director of Hong Kong Disneyland for eight years, joined Wanda to head its theme park business. Kam left Disney in early 2016, shortly after Hong Kong Disneyland announced a net financial loss of US$19 million in fiscal year 2015 after three years of gains. The conflict between Wanda and Disney escalated when performers dressed as Disney's characters Snow White and Captain America appeared at Nanchang Wanda

City. Disney warned Wanda that the company was prepared to take action to protect its intellectual property rights. However, Disney did not take former legal action in an attempt to avoid drama complicating the Shanghai Disneyland opening. Wanda defended itself by saying that it was not the company's idea but a spontaneous measure by the retailers in the complex outside of the park, not inside the park. In response to the fake Disney character incident, Wanda released a statement: "Wanda Group pays great attention to intellectual property protection and holds many registered cartoon trademarks."

Nanchang Wanda City was not the first local theme park in China that featured fake Disney characters. In 2007, Beijing state-owned Shijingshan Amusement Park replicated then two-year-old Hong Kong Disneyland with the slogan "Disneyland is too far, come to Shijingshan." Shijingshan featured a replica of Cinderella's Castle and was comprised of themed lands named Adventureland and Fantasyland, the same as those at Hong Kong Disneyland, with staff dressed as Mickey Mouse, Minnie Mouse, Snow White, and the other Disney characters. Although Wanda strongly positioned itself as a rival to Disney while Shijingshan simply exploited the Disney images to empower itself, both examples indicated the lack of popular original intellectual properties for local theme parks in a developing stage. On the contrary, Disney has a fully developed spectrum of stories and characters to leverage with, including classic images such as Mickey Mouse and Snow White, and new characters from Pixar, Marvel, and *Star Wars*.

Multinationals tend to perform well in the Chinese market because of their skills in consumer insights and branding that differentiate them from local competitors, which might be large in size and affluent in economic capital but are still developing world-class functional capabilities (Orr, 2014). China's first modern theme park, Splendid China, opened in Shenzhen in 1989, 34 years after the first Disneyland opened in Anaheim in 1955. According to the Themed Entertainment Association, in 2015, before Shanghai Disneyland opened, populous China had three theme parks ranked among the world's top 25 most-visited parks, including Chimelong Ocean Kingdom in Zhuhai (Guangdong province) ranked as 13th with about 7.5 million visitors, Hangzhou Songcheng Park in Hangzhou (Zhejiang province) ranked as 17th with about 7.3 million visitors, and Songcheng Lijiang Romance Park in Lijiang (Yunnan province) ranked as 25th with about 4.7 million visitors. However, the theme park industry in China was, in general, in the developing stage. Such status gave Disney and the other foreign cultural companies a chance to crack into the Chinese market under the condition of sharing their experiences for the local to grow.

The Chinese government allowed Disney to hold 70 percent of the shares in the management company because the country was eager to learn Disney's experience in managing theme parks to advance the local tourism industry. Other than Disney's rich storytelling, many believe that Disney has set a new benchmark for local industries to create higher-standard resorts with a strong emphasis on quality, innovation, and safety. As stated in Chinese President Xi's congratulatory letter for the opening of Shanghai Disneyland, "Disney style" and its "international standard" were esteemed by the local. Gas, former general manager of Shanghai Disneyland, further emphasized the importance of playing along with the Chinese party–state's agenda to help the country develop the tourism industry and the service sector:

> "One of the most exhilarating missions that the CEO, Robert Iger, gave me was to think of this as not only building the business but also helping the country raise its level… it is about our role within this overall Chinese agenda, which I think is great."
>
> (Nunlist, 2016)

Incubating the local cultural industries through the collaboration with global players used to be a hidden agenda for the Chinese government (Fung, 2008). However, for Shanghai Disneyland, developing the local industry is not a hidden agenda but one of the terms in negotiation on table.

In exchange for the tremendous business potential in China, Disney is willing to share its cultural capital. An example is the Beijing Animation Center, co-established by Disney, China's Ministry of Culture, and China's largest Internet company Tencent Holdings Ltd., to develop local animation content, through sharing Disney's storytelling ability and animation production skills. To profit from the affluent Chinese market, major global cultural players accept terms they would not compromise in the other markets, even knowing that the Chinese government is learning from foreign companies to bolster the country's own cultural industries. Shanghai Disneyland witnessed how Disney learned to compromise over time. In the beginning, Disney held a strong position about launching Disney Channel in China as a condition of the park's opening. For the company, Disney Channel not only drives direct revenue but is also essential to educating the Chinese audience about Disney's intellectual properties so that they have enough understanding and appreciation to visit Disneyland and consume Disney's products. Over the years, Disney learned the difficulty for the Chinese party–state to approve a foreign television channel in China, especially a kid's channel that might "poison" the young generation. Disney decided to drop the Disney Channel condition when the company found a way to justify itself by identifying new media and films as alternative sites to create brand awareness and brand affinity. Walt Disney's "secret" to making dreams come true was summarized as the four Cs: curiosity, confidence, courage, and constancy (Eddy, 2006: 55). In the case of Shanghai Disneyland, Disney's "secret" has expanded to five Cs with "compromise."

Government relations

When being asked about major business challenges in China, all of my Disney informants highlighted government regulations. Likewise, in a China Business Climate Survey Report released in early 2017 by The American Chamber of Commerce in China, three of the top five business challenges in China its American member companies identified were policy-related, including inconsistent regulatory interpretation and unclear laws, increasing Chinese protectionism, and difficulty obtaining required licenses to run business. Unclearness of regulations creates gray areas where the Chinese officials are authorized to interpret the text based on their personal understandings. As a result, major foreign cultural companies in China are cultivated to orchestrate with the party–state's agenda and place a great emphasis on government relations. Disney is not exempted, especially after a few lessons learned in China over the years, such as the movie release of *Kundun* in 1997, and the over-the-top service of DisneyLife in 2016.

Directed by Martin Scorsese and produced by Disney's Touchstone Pictures, *Kundun* (1997) is a pro-Tibet, anti-Communist biographical movie about the exiled 14th Dalai Lama. Following the reincarnation of the two-year-old Dalai Lama to his exile to India in 1959, this film conveyed strong anti-CCP messages, such as Chairman Mao's comments on how Tibetans were poisoned by opium-like religion, and the CCP's military crush of the religious and political traditions in Tibet. The release of *Kundun* irritated the CCP. The Chinese government ordered all lines of Disney's business in China to be shut down, including rejecting the release of Disney's pro-China movie *Mulan* (1998), Disney's first animated feature based on an Asian story. "All of our business in China stopped overnight," said Michael Eisner, Disney's then chief executive officer (Barboza & Barnes, 2016).

To manage the *Kundun* crisis, Disney hired former Secretary of the United States Henry Kissinger to intensely lobby with the Chinese officials in October 1997 (Yu, 2014). When Disney's then chief executive officer Michael Eisner finally had a chance to meet then Chinese Premiere Zhu Rongji, Eisner apologized to Zhu by summarizing the release of *Kundun* as a mistake. Although *Mulan* was finally released in China after the lobbying, in the end, this movie only fulfilled one-sixth of Disney's box office projections. The *Kundun* "mistake" taught Disney to compromise under the context of "socialism with Chinese characteristics" and carefully play along with the Chinese party–state's agenda. Since then, Disney has been enhancing its relations with the Chinese government and intensifying its localization efforts.

Another lesson for Disney is DisneyLife, Disney's over-the-top (OTT) services partnered with China's major digital player Alibaba Group Holding Limited, the world's largest online mobile commerce company, to tap into cord-cutters. Launched on December 15, 2015, DisneyLife was a Mickey Mouse head-shaped device connecting to television that enabled Chinese audiences to stream Disney's content of movies, series, e-books, games, Disney theme parks information, and travel services. The launch of DisneyLife was a major milestone for the company to have a virtual Disney Channel connecting to millions of the digital population in China, the world's largest Internet market. In the 38th China Internet Network Development Report released by China Internet Network Information Center, China Internet users reached 710 million in June 2016, over 50 percent of the national population. Among them, 30.4 percent were aged 20–29, 24.2 percent were aged 30–39, and 20.1 percent were aged 10–19. On an average, weekly Internet use time was 26.5 hours, i.e., 3.8 hours per day. Online video viewers reached 514 million, online consumers 448 million, and online gamers 391 million.

While Disney was celebrating its digital breakthrough of DisneyLife with another round of vibrant marketing campaign to promote the new colors of the Mickey Mouse-shaped OTT device, the Chinese government unexpectedly forced DisneyLife offline. It was only five months after the services were provided. The reason of the short lifespan of DisneyLife was said to be the Chinese party–state's increasing awareness of monitoring digital content. Disney perceived the cutoff, months before the Shanghai Disneyland opening, as a signal that demanded the company to revisit and strengthen its relations with the Chinese government.

Disney has a dedicated Department of Government Affairs in China to deliver "targeted advocacy in support of business goals" and to signify the company's "commitment to its strategic relationships with key policy makers and government officials" (PR Newswire, 2010). Back in April 1996, Disney's executives secured a meeting with then Chinese

President Jiang Zemin to pursue mutual interests in the market (Yu, 2014). On May 5, 2016, the day before Shanghai Disneyland's six-week trial operation period, Xi met with Iger, who was identified as "vice chair of US–China Business Council (USCBC) and chairman and chief executive officer of the Walt Disney Company," as China's Central Television reported. In this meeting, Xi applauded both the USCBC and The Walt Disney Company for their efforts in boosting bilateral relations with China. Iger then stressed how Disney attached great importance to promoting the culture exchanges between the United States and China. This meeting suggested political backing for Shanghai Disneyland. "I voted yes for Disney," Xi said, "because China needs a diverse-culture-based entertainment market" (Xinhua, 2016).

Corporate communications, corporate responsibility, and corporate outreach programs are part of Disney Government Affairs' tasks. In addition to carefully playing along with the Chinese government's agenda, Disney has learned not to offend the party–state by unnecessary news releases. Take two reports in the Shanghai-based, party-oriented newspaper *Jiefang Daily* for example. On February 9, 2006, Disney's executives confirmed that Disney was in talk with the Shanghai government for the construction of the Shanghai Disney Resort. However, one month later on March 7, Disney officially denied it. One of the reasons was believed to be the pressure from the Chinese government because Disney seemed an avaricious capitalist to have talked about another Disneyland soon after the September 2005 opening of Hong Kong Disneyland.

For global cultural companies, promoting Chinese culture is crucial to maintaining relations with the Chinese government. For example, in early 2017, Shanghai Disneyland celebrated its first Chinese New Year of the Rooster with festival decorations, dragon dance performances, a daily drum ceremony, and Mickey Mouse and friends in Chinese costumes greeting the audience. In addition to the domestic events, Disney commits to helping its local Chinese partners to expand internationally with an endorsement of local cultural superiority, a political agenda to realize the China Dream initiated by Chinese President Xi Jinping in November 2012 for the great rejuvenation of the Chinese nation. An example of such a commitment is the preschooler animated series *P. King Duckling,* produced by UYoung, a Chinese studio in Beijing. In 2015, UYoung successfully exported this series to Disney Junior channels for a global rollout in the United States, Latin America, India, Korea, and South East Asia. Cultural flows are not simple one-ways. Counter-flows exist for non-Western countries to export their cultures to the global market. U Young's *P. King Duckling* is an example of such a counter-flow.

Through the examinations of Tokyo Disneyland and Hong Kong Disneyland, Lee and Fung (2013) summarized Disneyland's five strategies: First, synergy across various business lines for cross-promotion; second, encouragement of consumption and commodification; third, careful calculation of entrance admission as either unaffordable or cheap; fourth, recycles of old materials by blending classic Disney characters with modern characters; and fifth, global expansion to build Disneyland in populous, global cities. All these strategies are valid for Shanghai Disneyland. However, in China, denial of access to the lucrative Chinese market is the party–state's highhanded measure to force global capitals to comply with the government's interests. As a result, on top of the above five strategies, Disney's ultimate strategy in China is maintaining valuable government relations because there will be no business in which to exercise any strategy if the party–state blocks or suspends Disney's practices, which is not uncommon in the Chinese market.

Transforming the traditional central–peripheral roles

Different from the Western contexts in which the media have relative autonomy, in China, state control predominates. Ever since the CCP first allowed overseas companies into the country in the late 1970s, global companies have been cultivated to follow the party–state's rules. It is even so when China is empowered by the size of its market as the second largest economy in the world. As China accumulates its economic capital, the state is getting more powerful in asserting its demands by pressuring foreign cultural companies to increase their investments while sharing storytelling and technological advances at the same time to promote the country's development goals, even if that grooms local rivals for the foreign entities.

The capitalist mode of production has been divorced from its historical origin in the West (Dirlik, 1994). Non-Western countries are gradually empowered by economic prosperity with new self-confidence to develop their own cultural aspirations, which implies a shifting or destruction of centers when homogenizing forces are absorbed into the local and heterogenized through indigenization (Appadurai, 1990; Ang, 2001). Empowered by its market size and economic capital, China is transforming the traditional central–peripheral roles. Ownership in the economic capital sense of Hong Kong Disneyland and Shanghai Disneyland is an example of the ambiguous central–peripheral power play. In each case, Disney is the minority party that owns less than 50 percent, while the Chinese counterpart holds the majority of interests.

Gramsci's idea of hegemony (1933) argues that the groups with different interests and values have to engage in negotiations in order to result in genuine accommodation. The shift of a system is not to reject the system and all its items, but to re-articulate it. Based on consent rather than coercion, hegemony is maintained through ongoing articulation of opposing interests into the political affiliations of the hegemonic group. Following the Chinese government's policy to protect the local tourism industry, Disney holds the minority ownership in the owner companies of Shanghai Disneyland. To play along with the party–state's agenda to grow the local service sector, Disney owns the majority in the management company of Shanghai Disneyland to share its expertise in exchange for management fees and, more importantly, for positive government relations. Such an ownership structure creates an opportunity for both the Chinese party–state and Disney to accumulate their capitals. For China, Shanghai Disneyland is an asset to leverage the country's market potential to reproduce both economic capital by sharing the park revenues and cultural capital through acquiring Disney's world-class knowledge about theme park management. For Disney, Shanghai Disneyland provides an opportunity to maximize the company's business potential in China and minimize the financial risk as the minority ownership holder in the relatively unpredictable investment environment with Chinese bureaucratic characteristics.

To maximize organization profits, the global cultures are often trans-cultured for local agenda (Chan & Ma, 2002). The model of one-way cultural imperialism or localization is not comprehensive enough to study cultural conglomerates like Disney. As Disney's former chief executive officer Robert Iger put it, "The creation of the park (Shanghai Disneyland) was an education in geopolitics, and a constant balancing act of the possibilities of global expansion and the perils of cultural imperialism" (Iger, 2019: x). One concept that better illustrates the dynamics between a global company and a local market is glocalization, roughly meaning global localization. It was first used by Japanese economists in the 1980s. Glocalization in Japanese is *dochakuka*, meaning living on one's own land, originally an agricultural idea of adjusting one's farming techniques to local specifications for business gains. In Japan, such a concept of global localization is often attributed to Sony Corporation's former chief executive officer Akio Morita, who employed this concept in Sony's branding strategies in the 1980s and 1990s. In marketing terms, it means the tailoring of global products and services to suit particular cultural tastes.

The term glocalization was popularized by Roland Robertson (1992, 1994, 1995), one of the pioneering sociologist in the study of globalization, to explicate the heterogenization aspects of globalization. Rather than focusing on the Japanese perception of glocalization, Robertson generalizes this concept to discuss worldly local–global dynamics with an intention to abolish the opposition between the global and the local. Robertson argues that the notion of globalization is not inevitably in conflict with the idea of localization. Instead, globalization as the compression of the world with an accelerated pace of contacts among peoples and cultures has increasingly incorporated and reconstructed locality which reinforces localism. In this sense, locality is a standard component of globalization. In other words, globalization in the 20th century involves the particularization of universalism and the universalization of particularism when the processes of both globalization and localization thrive simultaneously despite their appearing contradictory. In short, as Kraidy (2003) argues, the global and the local are complementary competitors feeding off of each other.

In consumer culture, glocalization is deemed as a strategy among transnational and multinational corporations to sell their products with diversity under increasing global–local dynamics. Robertson (1994) points out that glocalization involves the construction of increasingly differentiated consumers and serves as an important basis for consumers' cultural capital formation. Both minor modifications to global products and major changes to those products for a specific local market are reflections of glocalization, which points to the significant overlap of the global and the local. In Hannerz's words (1990: 237), global culture is constituted by the "increasing interconnectedness of varied local cultures." Such interplay between micro-globalization and macro-localization is so prevailing that some argue that all globalization is ultimately a process of glocalization (Bryman, 2004).

Global capitalism is conditioned by cultural heterogeneity and cultural homogeneity. The rise of the word glocal or its process of glocalization indicates a dissolution of the local–global binary contrast. It is never a one-way imposition. Thus, with the notion of glocalization, a globalizing country has a chance to acquire the global powers to export its cultural products with local characteristics instead of being colonized. As a reflexive form of contemporary globalization, glocalization works as a strategy used by a transnational cultural company eyeing on the global market with a belief that diversity sells. Thus, business entities are increasingly local and intensely global at the same time.

Glocalization is a valid concept by which to study global entertainment players. For example, Disney's animated feature *Mulan* (1998) is believed to be a glocalization effort that combines the global market with local situations (Yu, 2014). Furthermore, glocalization is argued to be the core that transformed the indebted "cultural Chernobyl" Euro Disneyland to a better performer of Disneyland Paris. Glocalization also eased the crisis of low attendance for Hong Kong Disneyland through the adaptation to local visitors' customs, and adaptation of labor practices (Matusitz, 2010, 2011).

In China, capital is tremendously under state control. The ownership structure of Shanghai Disneyland, which is constituted by both local and global capitals, suggests not only glocalization, but *state-capital-led glocalization*: glocalization led by economic capital *of* the state (direct investment) and economic capital *with* the state (market potential). It is state-capital-led because Chinese state capital plays the major role in the state-owned joint-venture owner companies, and maintaining government relations is the top strategy for the global company, Disney, to maximize potential economic returns on its investment in the Chinese market.

Bibliography

Ang, I. (2001). Desperately guarding borders: Media globalization, 'cultural imperialism' and the rise of 'Asia'. In Yoa, S. (Ed.), *House of glass: Culture, modernity and the state in Southeast Asia*, 27–45. Singapore: Institute of Southeast Asian Studies.

Appadurai, A. (1990). Disjuncture and difference in the global cultural economy. *Theory, Culture & Society*, 7, 295–310.

Barboza, D. & Barnes, B. (2016, June 14). How China won the keys to Disney's Magic Kingdom. *The New York Times*. Retrieved January 12, 2020, from https://www.nytimes.com/2016/06/15/business/international/china-disney.html?_r=0.

Bryman, A. (2004). *The Disneyization of society*. London: SAGE Publications Ltd.

Chan, J. & Ma, E. (2002). Transculturating modernity. In Chan, J. & McIntyre, E. (Ed.), *In search of boundaries: Communication, nation-state and cultural identities*, 1–18. Westport, CT: Ablex.

Choi, K. (2010). Constructing a decolonized world city for consumption: Discourses on Hong Kong Disneyland and their implications. *Social Semiotics*, 20(5), 573–592.

Dirlik, A. (1994). *After the revolution: Waking to global capitalism*. London: Wesleyan University Press.

Eddy, D. (2006). The amazing secret of Walt Disney. In Jackson, K. (Ed.), *Walt Disney: Conversations*, 42–56. Oxford, MS: University Press of Mississippi.

Fung, A. (2008). *Global capital, local culture: Transnational media corporations in China*. New York: Peter Lang.

Gramsci, A. (1933/1992). *Prison notebooks*. New York: Columbia University Press.

Griswold, W. (2003). *Cultures and societies in a changing world*. Thousand Oaks: Pine Forge.

Hannerz, U. (1990). Cosmopolitans and locals in world culture. In Featherstone, M. (Ed.), *Global Culture*, 237–252. London: SAGE Publications Ltd.

Iger, R. (2019). *The ride of a lifetime: Lessons learned from 15 years as CEO of the Walt Disney Company*. New York: Random House.

Kraidy. M.M. (2003). Glocalization as an international communication framework? *Journal of International Communication*, 9(2), 29–49.

Lee, F. (2009). Cultural discount of cinematic achievement: The academy and U.S. movies' East Asian box office. *Journal of Cultural Economics*, 33(4), 239–262.

Lee, M. & Fung, A. (2013). One region, two modernities: Disneyland in Tokyo and Hong Kong. In Anthony Y.H. Fung (Ed.), *Asian popular culture: The global (dis)continuity*, 42–58. New York: Routledge.

Matusitz, J. (2010). Disneyland Paris: A case analysis demonstrating how glocalization works. *Journal of Strategic Marketing*, 18(3), 223–237.

Matusitz, J. (2011). Disney's successful adaptation in Hong Kong: A glocalization perspective. *Asia Pacific Journal of Management*, 28(4), 667–681.

PR Newswire (2010, March 24). The Walt Disney company appoints Yvonne Pei Senior Vice President, Government Affairs, Greater China. *PRNewswire*. Retrieved January 15, 2020, from http://en.prnasia.com/story/29350-0.shtml.

Kuo, Y. (2016, January 4). 3 great forces changing China's consumer market. *World Economic Forum*. Retrieved January 18, 2020, from https://www.weforum.org/agenda/2016/01/3-great-forces-changing-chinas-consumer-market/.

Ren, H.L. (2016, June 16). Disney's China dream (in Chinese). *Xinmin Weekly*, 24, 8–15.

Robertson, R. (1992). *Globalization: Social theory and global culture*. London: SAGE Publications Ltd.

Robertson, R. (1994). Globalization or glocalization. *The Journal of International Communication*, 1(1), 33–52.

Robertson, R. (1995). Glocalization: Time-space and homogeneity-heterogeneity. In Featherstone, M., Lash, S. & Robertson, R. (Ed.), *Global modernities*. London: SAGE Publications Ltd.

Solomon, F. (2017, February 9). Disney CEO Bob Iger: A trade war with China would hurt us. *Fortune*. Retrieved January 12, 2020, from http://fortune.com/2017/02/09/disney-iger-trump-china-trade-war/.

Xinhua. (2016, January 14). Disney names day for city opening. *Shanghai Daily*. Retrieved January 15, 2020, from https://archive.shine.cn/metro/entertainment-and-culture/Disney-park-to-boost-Shanghai-economy/shdaily.shtml.

Yu, H. (2014). From Kundun to Mulan: A political economic case study of Disney and China. *Asia Network Exchange*, 22(1), 13–22.

4 Construction of local identities for Shanghai Disneyland

Since the construction stage, Shanghai Disneyland has been promoted as "authentically Disney and distinctly Chinese," a creative direction initiated by Disney's then chief executive officer Robert Iger. On the day before the Shanghai Disneyland opening, Iger further emphasized that Shanghai Disneyland was not just Disneyland in China, but "China's Disneyland" (Levine, 2016). Phillipe Gas, then general manager of Shanghai Disneyland added, "We want to be a citizen of Shanghai, and we have been" (Nunlist, 2016). Shanghai Disneyland is, so far, the only Disneyland for which Disney constructed local identities from the moment the project was approved (Table 4.1). Before further examining such identities, I will first turn to the other Disneyland outside of the United States: Tokyo Disneyland, Disneyland Paris, and Hong Kong Disneyland, to understand the differences of Shanghai Disneyland and how Disney built Shanghai Disneyland based on experiences generated from these earlier parks.

Identities of overseas Disneyland: Tokyo, Paris, Hong Kong, and Shanghai

As Disney's former chief executive officer Robert Iger put it, Shanghai Disneyland is a learning outcome which "combines all the things we have learned over the years from all the other parks we have operated... In a way, it's the smartest park we've ever built, based on our own learning" (Palmeri, 2016). Philippe Gas, former general manager of Shanghai Disneyland, also stated, "It is part of a journey of development, understanding what to do to succeed in different contexts and different markets. So we have taken all that to make this product" (Nunlist, 2016).

46 *Construction of local identities for Shanghai Disneyland*

Table 4.1 Identity of Disneyland outside of the United States

Park	General identity	Local identity
Tokyo Disneyland, Japan	Real Disneyland	Nonapplicable
Disneyland Paris, France	Magic Kingdom	Nonapplicable
Hong Kong Disneyland, China	Wholesome family entertainment	Nonapplicable
Shanghai Disneyland, China	Authentically Disney and distinctly Chinese	China's Disneyland; a citizen of Shanghai

Tokyo Disneyland

Opened on April 15, 1983, Tokyo Disneyland is a Japanese imagination of the Americanized "real Disneyland" (Brannen, 1992; Raz, 1999). Disney's local partner, Oriental Land Co., Ltd., which owned 100 percent of Tokyo Disneyland, advised Disney that the local audience preferred real Disneyland to a Japanese version of Disneyland. In other words, for Tokyo Disneyland, foreignness was an advantage, not a threat. To meet the local audience's expectations, Tokyo Disneyland, although owned and operated by the Japanese, has been constructed as an American original.

Such an original American identity is reflected in the park's dedication plaque:

> "To all of you who come to this happy place, welcome. Here you will discover enchanted lands of Fantasy and Adventure, Yesterday and Tomorrow. May Tokyo Disneyland be an eternal source of joy, laughter, inspiration, and imagination to the peoples of the world. And may this magical kingdom be an enduring symbol of the spirit of cooperation and friendship between the great nations of Japan and the United States of America."

The first sentence of the dedication is a standard opening originated from the first Disneyland in the United States. The second denotes the themed lands of Fantasyland, Adventureland, and Tomorrowland featured at the original Disneyland in Anaheim. The third discloses what Disney signifies: joy, laughter, inspiration, and imagination. The last sentence literally states the keywords of Americanized Disneyland the Japanese preferred: magical kingdom and United States, an epithet for Disney.

Disneyland Paris

Drawing on the popularity of Tokyo Disneyland, Disney applied the Japanese model to open Euro Disney (later named Disneyland Paris) as Americanized Disneyland on April 12, 1992. The park's dedication strongly encodes its American origin while emphasizing its connection with Europe:

> "To all who come to this happy place, welcome. Once upon a time... a master storyteller, Walt Disney, inspired by Europe's best loved tales, used his own special gifts to share them with the world. He envisioned a Magic Kingdom where these stories would come to life, and called it Disneyland. Now his dream returns to the lands that inspired it. Euro Disneyland is dedicated to the young and the young at heart... with a hope that it will be a source of joy and inspiration for all the world."

The first and the last sentences of this dedication are identical with those from the first Disneyland in the United States. The second to the fourth highlight the connection between Disneyland and Europe.

The general sentiment among the Europeans, however, was different from that of the Japanese. Euro Disney was criticized as a "cultural Chernobyl" that excluded local preferences, caused workers to protest against Disney's dress code, and led to years of financial losses (Matusitz, 2010). To improve the park's business performance, Disney gradually infused French references, such as the replacement of the first American general manager with a French-born executive and the offering of French wine at Disneyland Paris although alcohol was originally a taboo at sanitized Disneyland.

Hong Kong Disneyland

Disneyland Paris showed Disney the inadequacy of reproducing Americanized Disneyland without considering local tastes. However, Hong Kong Disneyland, which opened on September 12, 2005, is a replica of the original Disneyland in the United States for a couple of reasons. First, Hong Kong was deemed as an Asian city like Tokyo and it was assumed that the audience in the same region shared consonant aspiration. Second, due to the financial loss at Disneyland Paris, Disney tried to minimize its investments, in terms of both economic capital and time for innovation.

For wholesome family entertainment, Disney rejected the Hong Kong government's idea to broadly reflect the Chinese culture by arguing the importance of a genuine Disney experience, a formula proven successful at Tokyo Disneyland (Slater, 1999). The dedication of Hong Kong Disneyland resembled that of Tokyo Disneyland:

> "To all who come to this happy place, welcome. Many years ago, Walt Disney introduced the world to enchanted realms of fantasy and adventure, yesterday and tomorrow, in a magical place called Disneyland. Today that spirit of imagination and discovery comes to life in Hong Kong. Hong Kong Disneyland is dedicated to the young and the young at heart... with the hope that it will be a source of joy and inspiration, and an enduring symbol of the cooperation, friendship and understanding between the people of Hong Kong and the United States of America."

From the opening day, Hong Kong Disneyland was criticized for its disregarding local customs. In October 2005, one month after the opening, local audiences were irritated by how Hong Kong Disneyland asked the local police inspectors to remove cap and badge before conducting official duties to avoid spoiling the experiences of the other visitors in the park. The biggest conflict was the ticketing fiasco in 2006 during the Chinese New Year when Hong Kong Disneyland underestimated the number of tourists. More visitors than the maximum daily capacity arrived during this most celebrated Chinese festival. For safety reasons, Hong Kong Disneyland closed its gates to ticket holders. Hundreds of angry visitors shouted over the fence. Apologies from Disney's executives did not stop public criticism.

The company's incapability to manage its staff and the visitors at Hong Kong Disneyland had been under scrutiny. On the second opening day, Hong Kong local newspaper *Ming Pao Daily* reported that some visitors disregarded the park's rules with a photo showing a woman in a Minnie cap smoking in an open area. The same report also featured a photograph of a woman helping a young child loosen his trousers to urinate beside a flowerbed. On the same day, *Apple Daily* had a similar photograph of another child urinating near one of the park's restaurants. In September 2006, one year after the park opening, *Oriental Daily News* reported how four Disney "cast members" (what Disney calls its staff) pulled off each other's coverings in the changing room of Hong Kong Disneyland. The park did not make any profit until year 2012, seven years after its opening. Disney was deemed as having a difficult translation of its Western theme park concept into Hong Kong.

Shanghai Disneyland

Disney learned from Disneyland Paris and Hong Kong Disneyland the importance of avoiding cultural missteps for better business performance. The company also observed the Chinese party–state's strong concerns about cultural imperialism over the decade-long negotiation of Shanghai Disneyland. To win the entrée, Disney made major concessions, such as dropping the Disney Channel condition, sharing extensively its entertainment expertise with the local partners, and creating brand new attractions for Shanghai Disneyland upon the Chinese officials' requests. Disney has been cultivated to conduct self-censorship in its business plans and press releases in China. From the construction stage, Shanghai Disneyland was carefully framed as a "distinctly Chinese" site. Robert Iger, former chief executive officer of The Walt Disney Company, emphasized his vision for Shanghai Disneyland as "integrating local elements throughout the park," and stated that "I very much wanted to avoid being called a cultural imperialist" (Shanghai Daily, 2016). Still, Chinese local concerns about Disney's cultural imperialism emerged because the country, with a strong awareness of its historical greatness, is sensitive about any imperialist attempt, and Disney is an easy target as one of the largest entertainment companies in the world.

One year before the opening of Shanghai Disneyland, the Themed Entertainment Association indicated in its 2015 Global Theme Parks Report that "the Chinese government is cautious about having too much Western content" in attractions. At the annual political meetings in Beijing in March 2016, Li Xiusong, a representative of the Chinese People's Political Consultative Committee from Anhui province, stressed that China should not allow too many Disney parks: "This will lead our kids to chase after Western culture at a young age... When they grow up, they will feel indifferent to Chinese culture" (Chang, 2016). What Li recommended was local parks and attractions inspired by Chinese classics such as *Journey to the West*, a popular 16th-century Chinese mythological novel.

An example of local theme parks with prominent Chinese appearances like Li recommended is Wanda City. As discussed in the previous chapter, Dalian Wanda Group's billionaire Chairman Wang Jianlin argued that Western Disney should not have come to China. He declared a patriotic war on Disney with an announcement to take down the "only tiger" Shanghai Disneyland with "a pack of wolves" of Wanda Cities that featured Chinese stories and architectures. Wang stressed that Disney had misread the Chinese market. He commented, "the frenzy of Mickey Mouse and Donald Duck and the era of blindly following them have passed" (Barboza & Barnes, 2016).

Echoing Wang's sentiments, local netizens expressed their concerns (Allen-Ebrahimian, 2016). "No matter what, with regard to Disney, I absolutely support Wang Jianlin... I do not plan to go to Disney," wrote a user in Weibo, China's microblogging services like American Twitter. Another user found Disney "boring" and argued that "China has a lot of good stories." Another commented, "The era in which American culture commands the globe is slowly changing... Once China becomes strong, it will be Chinese culture that is the world's mainstream culture."

Despite the social critics and doubts, the launch of "distinctly Chinese" Shanghai Disneyland was smooth as its carefully chosen opening date of June 16, 2016 suggested (the number "six" in Chinese indicates "smooth"). Phillipe Gas, then general manager of Shanghai Disneyland, said, "Six is a lucky number in China, and according to the Chinese calendar, it is the best date" (Xinhua, 2016). The local identities of Shanghai Disneyland that Disney had carefully constructed helped to keep the launch smooth. Shanghai Disneyland was free of incidents like the protests during the 1992 Disneyland Paris opening period, or the complaints following the 2005 Hong Kong Disneyland launch. The park attracted four million visitors in the first four months, higher attendance than any other Disneyland in its initial opening phase.

Drawing on earlier experiences of the other Disneyland, Disney constructed local identities for Shanghai Disneyland as an antidote to social critics of cultural imperialism for better government relations and audience engagement soon after the project was approved by the Chinese government. Through executive interviews and localized events, the park's local image was enhanced. From the park's construction stage, Disney's former chief executive officer Robert Iger told the press that Shanghai Disneyland would be "authentically Disney and distinctly Chinese." In addition to grooming a local image, this mandate serves to bring the Disney brand to China with a concession to local tastes, which functions as a sort of social orientation and a sense of one's place as Bourdieu (1984) argues.

The dedication plaque at Shanghai Disneyland is a material representation of its "distinctly Chinese" identity:

> "To all who come to this happy place, welcome. Shanghai Disneyland is your land. Here you leave today and discover imaginative worlds of fantasy, romance and adventure that will ignite the magical dreams within all of us. Shanghai Disneyland is authentically Disney and distinctly Chinese. It was created for everyone, bringing to life timeless characters and stories in a magical place that will be a source of joy, inspiration and memories for generations to come."

Iger further suggested a local identity of "China's Disneyland" for Shanghai Disneyland before the park opening: "I didn't want to build Disneyland in China. I wanted to build China's Disneyland... Not only could Chinese visitors relate to it, but they could be proud of it and could have a sense of ownership" (Levine, 2016). Philippe Gas, then general manager of Shanghai Disneyland, further stressed that Shanghai Disneyland exhibited Disney's long-term commitment in China as "a citizen of Shanghai": "We respect the rules of the game and the interest of the Chinese parties... We want to be a citizen of Shanghai and we have been, right from the opening day" (Nunlist, 2016). To further enhance the local image for Shanghai Disneyland, Gas stated in another interview that the park planned to hire 98 percent of its staff locally (He, 2017).

Another way to promote the local image for Shanghai Disneyland was through localized events, such as the Opening Eve Celebration, which highlighted the marriage of Disney expertise and Chinese culture. This two-hour celebration was broadcast nationwide on Dragon TV, a satellite television channel owned by state-owned Shanghai Media Group (SMG). The ceremony took place in front of Shanghai Disneyland's Enchanted Storybook Castle, Disney's largest castle in the world. Chinese composer Tan Dun, known for his film scores for *Crouching Tiger, Hidden Dragon* (2000), was invited to conduct the Shanghai Symphony Orchestra in performing his original composition for Shanghai Disneyland titled "Igniting the Magical Dream," which blends Chinese and Western music motifs along with iconic Disney music. Famous Chinese pianist Lang Lang, Shanghai Disneyland's "honorary ambassador," played on stage "Let It Go" from Disney's blockbuster animated feature *Frozen*, whose box office reached about US$50 million in China in 2014.

Local celebrities either performed Disney songs or shared their personal Disney experiences to endorse Shanghai Disneyland. In addition to the celebrities, an elderly male was invited to play Erhu (Chinese violin) side by side with a young girl playing violin with a choir of 800 members to highlight the park's multigenerational appeal and to further salute the fusion of Chinese and Western culture, the theme of the opening eve. An informant who attended this Opening Eve Celebration did not enjoy such fusion, especially when he heard the Chinese lyrics "oh castle" repeated in the theme song. He said, "I heard that the lyrics were originally written in Chinese. But they sounded like direct translations from English. After all, in Mandarin, who would literally sing an ode to a castle?" It is possible for an audience to operate with an oppositional code and decode a message in a contrary way (Hall,

1980). My informant's reaction was an example of an oppositional reading. In other words, local audiences do not necessarily appreciate producer Disney's localization efforts.

Localization of "The Chinese Walt Disney Company"

Building Shanghai Disneyland as "China's Disneyland" was not the first time Disney had constructed a Chinese identity to promote its business in China. The construction of local identities for Shanghai Disneyland was the outcome of learnings from Disney's earlier experiences in this market. When Stanley Cheung, former managing director of The Walt Disney Company (China) Ltd., joined the company in 2005, he proposed the concept of "The Chinese Walt Disney Company" as opposed to The Walt Disney Company in China. Similar to the construction of local identities for Shanghai Disneyland, Cheung's assertion of "The Chinese Walt Disney Company" served to win the local market and to demonstrate Disney's commitment to the Chinese government. To Cheung, simply dropping Disney's practices in the United States into China is "a narrow way of doing business," and "if that does not work, we do not have business" (China Daily, 2007). He proposed the following strategies: first, deepen the level of brand recognition, such as a Disney musical show to tour around China; second, create the entertainment programs tailored to local tastes, such as the establishment of a local content team; and third, develop new approaches to expand business scale and explore new business fields, such as acquiring local gaming developers (Fudan, 2009).

In July 2014, ten years into Cheung's tenure, Disney appointed a new managing director, Luke Kang, the former managing director of Disney Korea. In a talk in Beijing in 2015, Kang stressed an "Outside (Outward) In" approach. This terminology was not only to promote the Disney-Pixar movie *Inside Out*, which was scheduled to be released in China two weeks after the speech on July 30, but also to highlight the importance of the local context. That is, rather than planting Disney's inner culture into China, Disney was paying great attention to the outside Chinese context to adjust its local practices accordingly.

Kang summarized his three core strategies as locally appealing content, digital connections, and consumer engagement. One example of local relevance mentioned in the talk was the establishment of the Local Content team in 2012 to create content in local for local. Another example was the opening of the 53,000-square-foot Disney Store in Shanghai. The world's first Disney Store opened in 1987 in the Glendale Galleria in South California of the United States. The

Chinese store in the Lujiazui district of Shanghai is the first Disney Store in China and the largest one in the world. This store was opened on May 20, 2015 at 13:14, in hopes to constantly engage the local audience because 5201314 is homophonous in Mandarin with "I love you all my lifetime" to project anticipatory long-term commitment from the audience.

One of the factors global conglomerates tend to consider is cultural proximity, a characteristic predominately echoed in locally produced material based on language, ethnicity, religion, and other elements (Straubhaar, 1991). Both Cheung and Kang emphasized localization as an important strategy for Disney's business in China, which helps to resonate with the local audience, groom the local industry, promote cultural exchange, and enhance government relations. In addition to internal teams to create content in local with local for local, local partnership and stratified localization are two key localization strategies for "The Chinese Walt Disney Company."

Local partnership

Under the restrictions on media and entertainment in China, Disney's media division perceives local content through local partnership as the key to its local success. An example of China's regulations restricting global cultural content is the ban on foreign animation during prime time broadcasting. The first foreign animation introduced to China was Japan's *Astro Boy* series in 1981. Since then, a large amount of foreign animation has flooded into China, including China Central Television's broadcasting of 104 episodes of *Mickey Mouse and Donald Duck* over two years on Sunday evenings, beginning in October 1986. In 2000, a regulation issued by the State Administration of Radio, Film and Television (SARFT, 1998–2013), later named State Administration of Press, Publication, Radio, Film and Television and National Radio (2013–2018), and Television Administration (2018 onward), required local television stations to seek approval from SARFT under set quotas for imported animation to air on television. In 2004, SARFT issued another regulation to request that at least 60 percent of animation aired in a quarter be domestic.

In September 2006, SARFT announced a total ban on all foreign animation being broadcast during prime time, from 5 p.m. to 8 p.m., which largely decreased foreign animation on local television and endangered Disney's television program block *Dragon Club*. In May 2008, SARFT expanded prime time to 9 p.m., during which no foreign animation could be shown on all domestic cartoon channels and children channels. Since then, Disney's media division in China has been keen on local content creation. One of the early efforts made was *As the Bell Rings* adapted from Disney Channel's sitcom series. This local version featured Chinese local talents in local settings and was later developed into an animated version and a stage show at the 2010 Shanghai Expo.

To play along with the strict media regulations, Stanley Cheung, Disney China's former managing director, stated,

> "We have partnered with CCTV (China Central Television) on a variety of fronts and we want to make sure that what we do is actually consistent with the government's agenda, with what the people want, rather than what The Walt Disney Company wants. So that is going to make us different and make us The Chinese Walt Disney Company."
>
> (Tan, 2010)

In addition to traditional platforms, Disney partners with local digital players in China, as the local audience are migrating to the digital platform. At the end of 2013, Disney revealed a digital joint-venture plan with the SMG's BesTV digital subsidiary, which had the largest new media platforms in China, including IPTV, mobile TV, smartphones, and online streaming. This plan was to serve the Chinese audience who are increasingly connected to their viewing experiences across multiple platforms by combining the two companies' technology and marketing skills. To further tap into the digital population, in early 2016, Disney's sports channel, ESPN, teamed up with China's largest Internet company, Tencent. The multiyear deal offers American sports such as NBA games online on Tencent's QQ Sports site with Mandarin commentary and the recruitment of Chinese reporters and producers in China and in the United States.

Disney's theatrical division also relies on local partnership. As a remedy for the financial loss in the local film industry, the Chinese government first introduced the film revenue-sharing system with ten imported movies per year in 1994. In 2001, after China joined the World Trade Organization (WTO), the annual quota was raised to 20. In 2012, annual quota was further raised to 34 under an agreement signed with WTO. Through local partnership, Disney co-branded movies have a chance to qualify as local productions that are exempt from the import quota limitation. In 2014, Disney strengthened its partnership with state-owned SMG, China's second largest media group. Under a multiyear agreement, Disney and SMG planned to co-develop Disney-branded movies with Chinese elements for China and the other markets.

Overall, Disney's studio division in China develops local content in both short form and long form. The main purpose of the short form

Construction of local identities for Shanghai Disneyland 55

is to promote theatrical releases. For example, to market the 2016 animated feature *Finding Dory*, Disney worked with 1993-born Chinese swimmer celebrity Ning Zetao, who was named China's sports personality of year 2015, to make a 30-second video in which he swam with the movie's animated main character, blue tang fish Dory. Other than producing promotional videos featuring local celebrities, local landmarks provide another site for Disney to market its movies. For example, before the movie opening of *Star Wars: The Force Awakens* (2015), 500 Stormtroopers, iconic characters from the *Star Wars* series, were stationed on China's Great Wall to create movie awareness as most local audiences were not familiar with the *Star Wars* series.

Another example of Disney's movie localization is the Chinese translation of the plastic robot character Baymax from the 2014 animated feature *Big Hero Six*. In mainland China, Baymax is translated as Dabai (Big White), a name inspired by a local employee's pet, to match Baymax's appearance and resonate with the local audience. Moving beyond traditional direct translation, this new layer of locally relevant translation was believed to have contributed to *Big Hero Six*'s box office performance of over US$500 million in China, the best international box office for this movie.

Local promotions helped to make year 2016 a box office record year for Disney in China. Disney had four out of the five highest-grossing imported films and became the first Hollywood studio to make US$1 billion in a single year at the Chinese box office. Marvel's live-action movie *Captain America: Civil War* reached US$190 million at the box office in China, about one-fourth of the international performance. The Disney animated feature *Zootopia* reached US$235 million in China, again about one-fourth of the worldwide box office. In this movie, Disney incorporated a local character to increase cultural proximity: the anchor character in the Chinese version was a panda as opposed to the moose in the American version.

In terms of long-form theatrical content, in 2007, "The Chinese Walt Disney Company" co-produced its first Chinese movie, *The Secret of Magic Gourd*, with Beijing-based China Film Group. In 2009, in cooperation with the Wolong Giant Panda Nature Reserve in Sichuan, Disney's second Chinese movie, *Touch of the Panda*, was released. In 2010, Disney co-produced *High School Musical China* with SMG and Huayi Brothers Media Corporation. In December 2017, Disney partnered with SMG to produce *The Dreaming Man*, a Chinese-language remake of *The Proposal*, the 2009 Hollywood blockbuster romantic comedy.

In September 2020, Disney released the live-action version of *Mulan*. Although this movie was not led by the Disney China team, Disney changed this movie's opening castle to Shanghai Disneyland's Enchanted Castle. *Mulan* (2020) had generated high expectations in China since Disney announced its production, but criticism arose from the government and the netizens after its release. For example, the Chinese Communist Party's *Global Times* published a review, titled "poor artistic level, misunderstanding of Chinese culture lead to *Mulan* failure in China." The terms Disneyfication (Schickel, 1997) and Disneyization (Bryman, 2004) demonstrate a broad concern about Disney's soft power. The former refers to the sanitization and trivialization of products or events in an influential Disney way to assemble easily grasped smoothness, while the latter indicates the wide spread of Disney's principles to maximize consumers' willingness to purchase goods and services. In the absence of a local Chinese partner, Disney's *Mulan* (2020) witnessed another Disneyfied storytelling to cross-promote the company's even wider range of products when the "chi" emphasized throughout this movie echoed the "force" in the *Star Wars* series, and *Mulan*'s phoenix wing shot reminded the audience of the Marvel superheroes.

Disney's consumer products also rely heavily on local partners. In China, Disney does not own or operate any manufacturing plants but licenses its intellectual properties to local companies to manufacture Disney-branded products. The Company has an in-house creative team with local designers to provide design style guides to local licensees, including styles highlighting Chinese content, such as Mickey Mouse mooncakes and Chinese brush-painted Stormtroopers. As one of the world's most valuable brands, Disney has been highly controlling about its brand management. Disney's local licensees are requested to follow its International Labor Standards (ILS) program to avoid sweatshop or human rights controversy.

Disney launched its worldwide ILS program in 1996 after the first reports on sweatshop-like conditions appeared in 1995 about toymakers manufacturing Disney products. At that time, Disney had no full-time in-house compliance officer (Sethi, 2003). By the end of 2016, Disney ILS had 120 employees in 12 countries to improve working conditions in over 30,000 factories. About 28 percent of the factories for Disney's products were located in China. The program's manual highlights the Disney Code of Conduct for manufacturers and minimum compliance standards, sourcing restrictions, facility declaration and authorization, ILS audits, and ILS ethics policy. Disney's ILS is not only a manual for its consumer product licensees; it is applied to all Disney media and theatrical productions.

Published online, Disney's Code of Conduct for manufacturers specifies the prohibition of child labor, involuntary labor, subcontracting, coercion and harassment, and promotes nondiscrimination, health and safety, compensation, and protection of the environment. Child labor is strictly prohibited, with the term that "manufacturers will not use child labor." Here, "child" refers to a person younger than 15 (or 14 where local law allows) or, if higher, the local legal minimum age for employment or the age for completing compulsory education. To avoid sweatshops, reasonable compensation and working hours are emphasized. Violation of any of the standards will lead to termination of Disney's contracts. An example is the revocation in late 2016 of the licensing to Dongguan Qing Xi Juantiway Plastic Factory, a Chinese toymaker that violated labor standards.

Disney's consumer products are keen on localizing tangible goods to increase local relevance for better business performance. Festival products are prominent examples. For example, Disney character-shaped mooncakes for the Mid-Autumn Festival and Marvel-themed rice dumplings for the Dragon Boat Festival. Fashion is another category that tends to feature strong local flavor. One example is Mickey Mouse kungfu shoes partnered with Beijing Neiliansheng, China's time-honored shoe shop, which was established in 1853. This shop has been famous for making cloth shoes since the Ching Dynasty. Its products attracted government officials such as Chairman Mao and Deng Xiaoping. On the high-end, Disney works with local licensees to manufacture golden coins featuring Disney characters in accordance with particular Chinese zodiac signs for every Chinese New Year.

Stratified localization

"Diversity exists not only between cultures, but also within cultures" (Lie, 1997: 148). To win over the local audience for maximum profits, the global cultural players develop decentralizing strategies that make globalization more of a localization process (Giddens, 1999). Globalization is also associated with new dynamics of relocalization, as Robin (1991) argues, to insert a multiplicity of localities into an evolving global system. For Disney's business in China, one of the major challenges is the great extent of different tastes and various levels of disposable income in this populous country.

The top two-tier cites used to be Disney's main focus in China. An example was Disney English Learning centers, which were located in the tier-one and tier-two cities such as Shanghai, Beijing, Chengdu (Sichuan province), and Shenzhen. In recent years, the company has expanded its business to lower-tier cities in China. In 2016, Luke Kang, Disney China's managing director, told the press that he had turned his focus to tier three and four cities. It was predicted that half of the 46 million additional upper-middle-class and affluent households that would emerge in China by 2020 were likely to be located outside the top 100 cities (Kuo, 2016). As a result, stratified localization that attends to sophisticated local tastes is crucial for local success. For example, research showed that lower city-tiers preferred movie posters with prominent movie titles while top-two tiers preferred sophistication. Accordingly, Disney employed different designs for different city-tiers. For the company, localization is not only based on a general understanding of the local audience but also based on advanced studies of stratified locality in different city tiers.

The newly opened Shanghai Disneyland borrowed experiences from "The Chinese Walt Disney Company" to provide localized services. Shanghai Disneyland Merchandise conducted extensive research throughout China to talk with the audience about their tastes and interests. One finding about the local audience was that they preferred beautiful but, above all, practical products. For example, a Tinker Bell statue to be placed at home was less popular than a Tinker Bell printed T-shirt in the Chinese market. This finding was applied in the products provided at the park. David Koo, merchandise director of Shanghai Disneyland stated that "it all starts with understanding the consumer and creating the Disney-branded products they want. That means we work tirelessly together to research every product and supplier" (Yang, 2014).

Another study showed that the Chinese prefer Chinese food. As a result, 80 percent of the food at Shanghai Disneyland represents eight Chinese cuisines. When the park opened, Phillipe Gas, then general manager of Shanghai Disneyland emphasized that "there is only one place serving burgers (Nunlist, 2016)." Other than food, language is the most extensively localized to help the audience comprehend the text at Shanghai Disneyland. In terms of the use of the local language, Gas elaborated that it was not only about the final outcome presented on signs or in shows but from the development stage in Mandarin to generate locally relevant ideas. For example, the script of Frozen: A Sing-Along Celebration at Fantasyland was written in Chinese and the Western performers all spoke Mandarin on stage.

Reorientation of the cultural imperialism tradition

As one of the largest entertainment companies in the world, Disney is often criticized as promoting the imperialist ideology in order to exercise exploitative control over resources and people's beliefs, values, and behaviors through economic dominance. Imperialism, which is often used with negative connotation, invokes unequal relations of power. The concept of cultural imperialism emerged in the 1960s. It echoed the history of European colonial expansion that dominated and disrupted non-Western societies by arguing a post-imperial colonization by other means. Since the 1970s, in accordance with the Frank School's concerns about the media's threat to distort cultures and values, cultural imperialism and media imperialism have been largely employed to study the United States as a new kind of global power capable of dominating the world's economic, political, and cultural spheres to form cultural hegemony on a global scale.

Tomlinson (1991) perceives media imperialism as a way of talking about cultural imperialism. In his view, "imperialism grasps a specific form of domination, that associated with empire" (Tomlinson, 1991: 19). Cultural imperialism is also discussed as a critique of global capitalism, a homogenizing cultural force which unifies the look of the world and promotes a consumerist culture; as a discourse of nationality, which imposes the threat of cultural attack on the local culture of any nation; and as a critique of modernity, the main cultural direction of global development, which leads to homogenization of cultural diversity.

Drawing on dependency theory, which argues asymmetrical reliance and the unequal flow of resources from the poor peripheral to the wealthy core, Wallerstein's world system perspective (2011) expresses similar imperialism concerns. A world system does not necessarily encompass the entire globe but has global dimensions. By mapping out the world as a hierarchy of central, semi-peripheral, and peripheral, dominant capitalist core countries are criticized for exploiting peripheral countries for labor and raw materials. In the process, modern powers tend to justify their imperialist attempts by constructing a false image of the Other as barbarous and in need of civilization (Said, 1979). Among the core countries, the United States is viewed as the core of the core (Staniland, 1985).

Cultural companies equipped with strong economic capital are often under scrutiny for exercising cultural imperialism to reshape a society for the benefit of the imperial power. Joined by power and infantilization, reading innocence-packaged Disney content was described as "having one's own exploited condition rammed with honey down one's throat" (Dorfman & Mattelart, 1971: 98) to surrender to Disney ideology, which glorifies consumption in the "political utopia of a class" (Dorfman & Mattelart, 1971: 89) and portrays the Third World people as noble savages that should aspire to the superior

Western cultures. Building international Disneyland in Paris and Tokyo was criticized as an example of how American ideological assumptions were literally built into the architecture and landscape for cultural dominance (Schiller, 1991).

The cultural imperialism thesis draws great attention, as the dominated site might not be aware of the domination or even the erasure of local culture through such subtle, soft power. When local cultural distinctiveness is subsumed into global corporate culture, a society is at risk of losing its cultural identity and becoming an enslaved society (Crother, 2013). Disney's global expansion often generates fear and promotes resistance in a local site where Disney's products and norms appear to be powerful alien artifacts. In addition to negative connotation of the term Disneyfication or cultural imperialism, general suspicions about Disney arose: "The whole Walt Disney philosophy eats out of your hand with these pretty little sentimental creatures in grey fur coats... I believe that behind these smiling eyes there lurks a cold, ferocious beast, fearfully stalking us" (Baudrillard, 1988: 48).

In China, such imperialist concerns arise from the government officials, the industry, and the audience. Earlier learnings from the other Disneyland outside of the United States and from "The Chinese Walt Disney Company" helped Disney construct local identities for Shanghai Disneyland to enhance government relations and consumer engagement. Through executive interviews and localized events, Shanghai Disneyland has been constructed as "China's Disneyland," and "a citizen of Shanghai." As an institutional tactic, identity embodies politics to address issues of access or representation in order to protect and advance certain interests. Local identities help Disney to protect the company by avoiding social critics of cultural imperialism for a chance to survive in China and to advance the company's interests by increasing the park's relevance to the local audience.

Chen's concept of critical syncretism (2010) indicates a cultural strategy of identification for subaltern subject groups to interiorize elements of others to move beyond the boundaries constructed by colonial power relations. Here at Shanghai Disneyland, the subaltern is the minority ownership holder Disney that tries to seek alliances outside its limited frame. There is a reorientation of the media imperialism tradition and it is possible to have "a new media order reflective of the escalating power and influence of China" (Boyd-Barrett, 2015: 119).

Major producers of global culture increasingly tailor their products to differentiated global markets because embracing the differences in the local sites helps to sustain their business (Hall, 1997; Ang, 2001). For example, Coca Cola considered itself a "multi-local" company, not a "multi-national" company (Morley, 2006). Based on over one decade of local experiences, Disney has developed sophisticated localization strategies, such as local partnership and stratified localization. Under China's strong national protectionism and strict media policy, local partnership helps Disney to develop more co-branded products that are likely to qualify as local production with better distribution opportunities in the market. Moreover, diversity exists within cultures. Stratified localization attending to various local tastes in different city tiers increases Disney brand awareness and brand affinity to maximize the profit potential for the company.

In the case of Shanghai Disneyland, capitalism thrives on the contradictory direction of imperialist homogenized global culture. Homogeneity limits global cultural companies' profit potential in China, not only because diversity sells but also because homogeneity blocks the chance to enter the Chinese market. As a Disney informant shared, "We are too busy with the numbers (of revenues) to think about anything imperialism… Not to mention that we are lucky enough if the Chinese government does not shut our business down for whatever reasons… In China, 'local' is the key word."

Shanghai Disneyland's identities of being "authentically Disney and distinctly Chinese" and "China's Disneyland" encode politics to protect and advance Disney's interests in this US$5.5 billion project by avoiding the social critics of cultural imperialism to resonate with the local audience and, more importantly, to win entrée from the Chinese party–state. The phrasing of the park's identities that incorporate the word China and the word Disney is itself glocal. The main reason behind such a careful construction ever since the project was approved by the Chinese government is to gain the state's support to survive in the lucrative Chinese market. In other words, as with the ownership structure of Shanghai Disneyland, Disney's construction of local identities for Shanghai Disneyland indicates state-capital-led glocalization: glocalization led by economic capital *of* the state and economic capital *with* the state, to win both the state's investment and the local market.

Bibliography

Allen-Ebrahimian, B. (2016, June 16). Nationalist Chinese netizens are already turning on Disney Shanghai. *Foreign Policy*. Retrieved January 12, 2020, from https://foreignpolicy.com/2016/06/16/china-nationalists-disney-shanghai-wang-jianlin-wanda-mickey/.

Ang, I. (2001). Desperately guarding borders: Media globalization, 'cultural imperialism' and the rise of 'Asia'. In Yoa, S. (Ed.), *House of glass: Culture, modernity and the state in Southeast Asia*, 27–45. Singapore: Institute of Southeast Asian Studies.

Barboza, D. & Barnes, B. (2016, June 14). How China won the keys to Disney's Magic Kingdom. *The New York Times*. Retrieved January 12, 2020, from https://www.nytimes.com/2016/06/15/business/international/china-disney.html?_r=0.

Baudrillard, J. (1988). *America*. New York: Verso.

Bourdieu, P. (1984). *Distinction: A social critique of the judgment of taste*. London: Routledge and Kegan Paul.

Boyd-Barrett, O. (1977). Media imperialism: Towards an international framework for the analysis of media systems. In Curran, J. & Gurevitch, M. (Ed.), *Mass communication and society*, 116–135. London: Edward Arnold.

Boyd-Barrett, O. (2015). *Media imperialism*. London: SAGE Publications Ltd.

Brannen, M. (1992). Bwana Mickey: Constructing cultural consumption at Tokyo Disneyland. In Tobin, J. (Ed.), *Re-Made in Japan*, 216–235. New Haven: Yale University Press.

Bryman, A. (2004). *The Disneyization of society*. London: SAGE Publications Ltd.

Burton-Carvajal, J. (1994). Surprise package: Looking southward with Disney. In E. Smoodin (Ed.), *Disney discourse*, 131–147. New York: Routledge.

Chang, R. (2016, May 31). Disney sparks theme-park battle to entertain China's middle class. *Bloomberg*. Retrieved January 12, 2020, from https://www.bloomberg.com/news/articles/2016-05-30/disney-poised-to-spur-amusement-park-fun-in-land-of-dwarf-empire.

Chen, K.H. (2010). *Asia as method: Toward deimperialization*. Durham: Duke University Press.

China Daily (2007, June 25). Disney tackles China with traditional local tale. *China Daily*. Retrieved January 15, 2020, from https://www.chinadaily.com.cn/china/2007-06/25/content_901941.htm.

Crother, L. (2013). *Globalization and American popular culture*. Plymouth, UK: Rowen & Littlefield Publishers, Inc.

Dorfman, A. & Mattelart, A. (1971). *How to read Donald Duck: Imperialist ideology in the Disney comic*. Trans. D. Kunzle, New York: International General.

Fudan, (2009, November 13). 10 MBA students visited The Walt Disney Company (Shanghai) on November 10. *School of Management, Fudan University*. Retrieved January 15, 2020, from https://www.fdsm.fudan.edu.cn/en/aboutus/ShowNews.aspx?InfoGuid=0c7fad89-f4fc-41a0-84ef-333c4fea5ae5.

Giddens, A. (1999). *The consequences of modernity*. Cambridge: Polity Press.

Hall, S. (1980). Encoding/decoding. In Hall, S. et al. (Ed.), *Culture, media, language: Working papers in cultural studies, 1972–79*, 117–127. London: Hutchinson.

Hall, S. (1997). The local and the global: Globalization and ethnicity. In King, A. (Ed.), *Culture, globalization and the world-system*, 19–40. Minneapolis: The University of Minnesota University.
He, W. (2017, January 7). Shanghai Disney expands talent pool. *China Daily*. Retrieved January 15, 2020, from https://www.chinadaily.com.cn/business/2017-01/07/content_27887374.htm.
Kuo, Y. (2016, January 4). 3 great forces changing China's consumer market. *World Economic Forum*. Retrieved January 18, 2020, from https://www.weforum.org/agenda/2016/01/3-great-forces-changing-chinas-consumer-market/.
Levine, A. (2016, June 23). Bob Iger: Shanghai Disney isn't just Disneyland in China. *USA Today*. Retrieved January 15, 2020, from http://www.usatoday.com/story/travel/experience/america/2016/06/23/bob-iger-interview-shanghai-disney-resort-opening/86253624/.
Lie, R. (1997). What's new about cultural globalization? Linking the global from within the local. In J. Servaes and R. Lie (Ed.), *Media and politics in transition: Cultural identity in the age of globalization*, 141–155. Leuven: ACCO.
Matusitz, J. (2010). Disneyland Paris: A case analysis demonstrating how glocalization works. *Journal of Strategic Marketing*, 18(3), 223–237.
Morley, D. (2006). Globalisation and cultural imperialism reconsidered: Old questions in new disguise. In Curran, J. & Morley, D. (Ed.), *Media and cultural theory*, 30–43. New York: Routledge.
Nunlist, T. (2016, December 15). Behind the scenes in the Magic Kingdom. *CKGSB Knowledge*. Retrieved January 5, 2020, from https://knowledge.ckgsb.edu.cn/2016/12/15/conversations/shanghai-disney-resort-behind-scenes/.
Palmeri, C. (2016, June 13). Disney's foreign curse could end with China resort project. *Bloomberg*. Retrieved January 5, 2020, from https://www.bloomberg.com/news/articles/2016-06-12/disney-s-foreign-curse-could-end-with-5-5-billion-china-resort.
Raz, R. (1999). *Riding the black ship: Japan and Tokyo Disneyland*. Cambridge: Harvard University Asia Center.
Robin, K. (1991). Tradition and translation: National culture in its global context. In Corner, J. & Harvey, S. (Ed.), *Enterprise and heritage*. London: Routledge.
Said, E. (1979). *Orientalism*. New York: Random House.
Schickel, R. (1997). *The Disney version: The life, times, art and commerce of Walt Disney*. Chicago: Ivan R. Dee, Inc.
Schiller, H. (1973). *The mind managers*. Boston: Beacon Press.
Schiller, H. (1976). *Communication and cultural domination*. White Plains, New York: International Arts and Sciences Press.
Schiller, H. (1991). Not yet the post-imperialism era. *Critical Studies in Mass Communication*, 8(1), 13–28.
Sethi, S.P. (2003). *Setting global standards: Guidelines for creating codes of conduct in multinational corporations*. Hoboken, NJ: John Wiley.
Shanghai Daily (2016, July 13). Disney chief claims a million people visited park. *Shanghai Daily*. Retrieved January 12, 2020, from https://www.sohu.com/a/104993670_161402.

Slater, J. (1999). Aieeyaaa! A Mouse. *Far East Economic Review*, 162(45), 50–51.
Smith, A.D. (1995). *Nations and nationalism in a global era*. Oxford: Polity.
Smoodin, E. (1994). *Disney discourse*. New York: Routledge.
Staniland, M. (1985). *What is political economy? A study of social theory and underdevelopment*. New Haven, CT: Yale University Press.
Straubhaar, J. D. (1991). Beyond media imperialism: Assymetrical interdependence and cultural proximity. *Critical Studies in Mass Communication*, 8, 39–59.
Tan, K. (2010, June 15). Doing it the Chinese way: Disney's strategy for a lucrative ride in China. *Insead Knowledge*. Retrieved January 15, 2020, from http://knowledge.insead.edu/economics-politics/doing-it-the-chinese-way-1086.
Tomlinson, J. (1991). *Cultural imperialism: A critical introduction*. London: Printer.
Wallerstein, I. (2011[1974]). *The modern world-system: Capitalist agriculture and the origins of the European world-economy in the sixteenth century*. Berkeley and Los Angeles, CA: University of California Press.
Xinhua. (2016, January 14). Disney names day for city opening. *Shanghai Daily*. Retrieved January 12, 2020, from https://archive.shine.cn/metro/entertainment-and-culture/Disney-park-to-boost-Shanghai-economy/shdaily.shtml.
Yang, J. (2014, November 21). Tuning Disney themes to what shoppers want. *Shanghai Daily*. Retrieved January 15, 2020, from https://archive.shine.cn/feature/people/Tuning-Disney-themes-to-what-shoppers-want/shdaily.shtml.

5 "Distinctly Chinese" representations of Shanghai Disneyland

Opened on June 16, 2016, Shanghai Disneyland is part of Shanghai Disney Resort, which also features Disneytown, Walt Disney Grand Theater, Shanghai Disneyland Hotel, Toy Story Hotel, and Wishing Star Park, with a promenade and a lake across about 40 hectares (approximately 99 acres). Under the creative direction of being "authentically Disney and distinctly Chinese," Disney hired Chinese architects and designers to keep the iconic Disney characters but downplays direct Americanness and pays homage to the Chinese culture. In exchange for the maximum returns on its investment in Shanghai Disneyland, Disney attends to the Chinese local context carefully for the local visitors to groom a sense of ownership.

Inclusion and exclusion at Shanghai Disneyland

Shanghai Disneyland followed Walt Disney's original concept of the Disneyland layout: "Have a single entrance through which all the traffic would flow, then a hub off which the various areas were situated. That gives people a sense of orientation" (Smith, 2001: 54). Under such a design, visitors do not wander aimlessly but return continually along paths that have been walked, which ensures stability and encourages an intention to return (Clave, 2007; Urry, 1995).

There are seven themed lands and areas at Shanghai Disneyland: Mickey Avenue, Gardens of Imagination, Fantasyland, Adventure Isle, Treasure Cove, Tomorrowland, and its first major expansion in 2018, Disney-Pixar Toy Story Land (Figure 5.1). On December 15, 2019, Shanghai Disneyland announced the construction of its eighth themed land, Zootopia, the first Zootopia-themed land at a Disney park. Here, theming is a means of social interaction. It involves the use of story and technology to create entertainment that evokes a fantasy, a location, or an idea (Lukas, 2007).

66 *"Distinctly Chinese" representations of Shanghai Disneyland*

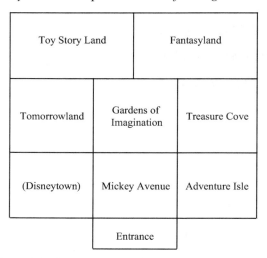

Figure 5.1 Themed lands at Shanghai Disneyland

Mickey Avenue

For Shanghai Disneyland, a Steamboat Mickey fountain, inspired by the first Mickey Mouse sound film released in 1928, is arranged at the entrance to greet the audience and propose prosperity as water suggests fortune in Chinese Feng Shui. In addition, the Steamboat fountain represents smooth sailing, as the Chinese idiom *yifanfengshun* indicates. The single entrance street at Shanghai Disneyland is Mickey Avenue, replacing the foreign concept of Main Street USA at Disneyland in the United States, Paris, and Hong Kong. Mickey Avenue is constructed as the toon hometown for Mickey Mouse and friends. This is the first time Disneyland presented a main entrance dedicated to Disney characters.

Renaming Main Street USA to Mickey Avenue has two purposes. First, similar to why Tokyo Disneyland changed the name of Main Street USA to World Bazaar (Yoshimoto, 1994), it is to avoid any trace of American nationalism that might not resonate with the local audience. In China, a further layer of avoidance is added to minimize the risk of irritating the party–state with any seemingly imperialist attempt. An effort made accordingly was to tailor park attractions for China and remove certain American trademark features. Second, the new name of Mickey Avenue increases local proximity because Chinese audiences are familiar with Mickey Mouse since its animated series premiered on China's Central Television in 1986. By downplaying the American connotation,

Disney hopes the local audience to embrace Shanghai Disneyland as China's own Disneyland for better business performance.

Mickey Avenue displays the spatial rationale of theme parks clustering commercial opportunities for consumption that endorse symbolic membership for self-construction and social approval (Davis, 1996; Zukin, 1991). Live entertainment, four restaurants and refreshment stands, including Mickey & Pal's Market Café, where local dim sum and noodles are served, and six gift shops are located on Mickey Avenue to encourage hybrid consumption of shopping, eating, and playing, interlocking with each other. Like Main Street USA, "a disguised supermarket" (Eco, 1986: 43), Mickey Avenue aims to give the pedestrian flaneurs ample space and opportunities to stroll, consume, and photograph with the costume characters of Mickey Mouse and friends.

Gardens of Imagination

Shanghai Disneyland's Mickey Avenue leads to worldwide Disneyland's first Gardens of Imagination, a seven-acre central hub with a collection of seven gardens. It is the first Disney-themed land designed as a garden and the first central plaza that includes a lagoon. This themed land was reported to be created to serve the growing local elderly population. According to the National Bureau of Statistics of China, in 2015, the number of people aged 60 and above reached 222 million, 16.1 percent of the total population in China; aged 65 and above reached 143.86 million, 10.5 percent of the total population. To emphasize this themed land's being "distinctly Chinese," John Sorenson, principal landscape architect at Walt Disney Imagineering Shanghai said,

> "A lot of trees you will see are familiar to most people in Shanghai, but we also tried to find unusual Chinese native trees... We spent a lot of time going to parts of the remote countryside of China (to find flora compatible with the climate in Shanghai)."
>
> (Tan, 2015)

Visitors not necessarily recognize any differences of the trees at the park. Such an effort of finding "unusual Chinese native trees" serves as another campaign of publicity to demonstrate Disney's localization commitment.

Chinese symbols are highlighted in the world's so-far one and only Garden of the Twelve Friends, where the twelve signs of the Chinese zodiac are depicted by Disney and Pixar characters in twelve walls of mosaic murals. The twelve characters selected are the mouse Remy from 2007's *Ratatouille*, Babe the Blue Ox from 1958's short *Paul*

Bunyan, the tiger Tigger from 1968's *Winnie the Pooh and the Blustery Day*, the rabbit Thumper from 1942's *Bambi*, the dragon Mushu from 1998's *Mulan*, the snake Kaa from 1967's *The Jungle Book*, the horse Maximus from 2010's *Tangled*, the Jolly Holiday Lambs from 1964's *Mary Poppins*, the monkey Abu from 1992's *Aladdin*, the rooster Alan-a-Dale from 1973's *Robin Hood*, Mickey's best puppy dog friend Pluto from 1930's *Silly Symphonies*, and the pig Hamm from 1995's *Toy Story*. Although these images seem too obscure to relate to the Chinese signs, Disney's localization efforts are appreciated when visitors take pictures with the mosaic murals of their corresponding Chinese signs.

Next to the Garden of the Twelve Friends is the Wandering Moon Teahouse which was reported to honor the creative spirit of Chinese poets. It serves Chinese cuisines, such as Shanghai pork belly rice and Fujian seafood noodles. The building itself stands for a collection of Chinese symbols. It recreates traditional three-storey Chinese architecture with red lanterns and ancient symbols from mountain, ocean, forest, and river. The rooms in the Wandering Moon Teahouse are designed to represent different areas of the country with Chinese poems in calligraphy on the walls. A couple in their 50s who visited Shanghai Disneyland shared with me their sentiment: "Unbelievable. We never imagined a Chinese building with couplets and red lanterns at Disneyland. We took a picture in front of this Teahouse and none of our friends believed that it was taken at Disneyland."

There are two rides in Gardens of Imagination: Dumbo the Flying Elephant, and the Fantasia Carousel. Unlike the original Disneyland's medieval-themed King Arthur Carousel, Shanghai Disneyland is the first Disneyland featuring horses inspired by the 1940 film *Fantasia* and a symphonic score. Around the Fantasia Carousel is The Fantasia Garden with flowering trees. Also featured in Gardens of Imagination is Marvel Universe, which exhibits popular superheroes such as Iron Man and Captain America. Ever since Disney acquired Marvel in 2009, Marvel has been an important asset for Disney. However, there is no Marvel ride but an exhibition hall at Shanghai Disneyland. The Marvel-themed rides are likely reserved for nearby Hong Kong Disneyland, which opened the world's first Marvel-themed Iron Man Experience ride in January 2017.

Fantasyland

In Walt Disney's view, fantasy could not become outdated because it represented a flight into a dimension that lied beyond the reach of time and nobody aged in this dimension. Walt believed that Disneyland

"Distinctly Chinese" representations of Shanghai Disneyland 69

"turned fairy tales fashionable again" and described Fantasyland as "a world of imagination, hopes and dreams ... dedicated to the young-in-heart, to those who believe that when you wish upon a star, your dreams come true" (Smith, 2001: 64). Walt's "never-outdated" Fantasyland is located in the center of all Disneyland.

At Shanghai Disneyland, Fantasyland is the largest themed land, anchored by the park's centerpiece castle. As Phillippe Gas, former general manager of Shanghai Disneyland, put it, "there must be a castle in the center of the park as the audience expects to see one at Disneyland" (Nunlist, 2016). However, Shanghai Disneyland has its local twists that are different from the other Disneyland castles. It is not the Cinderella Castle, the hub of American myths (Schultz, 1988), featured in Tokyo and Orlando, or the Sleeping Beauty Castle in Anaheim, Paris, and Hong Kong. At Shanghai Disneyland, it is the Enchanted Storybook Castle, the largest, tallest, and the most interactive Disneyland castle that represents all Disney princesses. The large scale of the castle is framed as Disney's statement to show respect to the Chinese government and the people of China (Hewitt, 2016). Encouraged by the success at Shanghai Disneyland, in 2019, Hong Kong Disneyland redesigned its Sleeping Beauty Castle to tribute several princesses.

The construction of Enchanted Storybook Castle began on May 25, 2013. Two years later, on May 19, 2015, a big celebration was held to highlight a special Chinese element in addition to the castle's large scale: it was topped with a golden peony, "the flower of China," according to a press released by Shanghai Disneyland. Under the peony are Disney stars signifying the partnership between Disney and China. The castle also includes Chinese design details of peonies, magnolias, and Chinese clouds, as well as local architecture details of jade columns and Chinese zodiac-inspired gargoyles. The golden "flower of China" is so high that no one is really tall enough to identify it. This peony topping of Disneyland's tallest castle in the world functions as a grand symbol to reinforce Shanghai Disneyland's local identity through publicity.

In addition to the Chinese elements in the design, the Enchanted Storybook Castle has several pioneering features. It is not only the tallest, at 196 feet, but also the first Disneyland castle for all princesses, with multiple main entrances from different sides. As an informant shared, one of the reasons why Shanghai Disneyland castle was not dedicated to one particular princess was because the local research could not identify any preferable princess among the local audience. This castle is also the most interactive Disneyland castle, including a walk-through attraction, a princess makeover boutique, a Royal Banquet

Hall restaurant with princess-centric dining rooms themed to Snow White, Aurora, Tiana, and Chinese-style Mulan, a stage for live performances, and The Voyage to the Crystal Grotto boat ride underneath the main level of the castle traveling through Fantasyland and passing scenes from Disney's animated features *Fantasia* (1940), *Beauty and the Beast* (1991), *Aladdin* (1992), *Mulan* (1998), and *Tangled* (2010). Predictably, Chinese Mulan is one of the park designer's favorite characters.

Inside this castle are marble statues of princesses along a helix staircase and mosaic murals depicting Tiana from *The Princess and the Frog* (2009), Rapunzel from *Tangled* (2010), Merida from *Brave* (2012), and Anna and Elsa from *Frozen* (2013) to represent the four seasons. Instead of classic Disney princesses, highlighted in the castle's mosaic murals are recent Disney princesses whom local audiences are more familiar with. The Once Upon a Time Adventure, a walk-through inside the castle equipped with the latest realistic interactive technology, is dedicated to Snow White. This attraction pays homage to Disney's first encounter with Shanghai, which hosted the *Snow White and Seven Dwarfs* (1937) Asian premiere as the first Disney property introduced to the Chinese audience.

Enchanted Storybook Castle features a nightly firework and laser show: Ignite the Dream – A Nighttime Spectacular of Magic and Light. Fireworks are the most popular shows at all Disneyland. For Disney's tallest castle at Shanghai Disneyland, the fireworks were reported either as reaching up to the waistline of the castle or causing noise pollution. Therefore, Shanghai Disneyland developed a 20-minute multimedia show featuring fireworks, projections, and lasers. This castle also hosts festival events. For the first Chinese New Year celebration at Shanghai Disneyland in 2017, a series of best wishes and quotes were projected onto Mickey Mouse-shaped lanterns on the castle. This interactive program was highlighted as "the first" among all Disneyland.

Near the castle is another first-ever attraction, the Alice in Wonderland Maze, which leads to the rides of Peter Pan's Flight, the Seven Dwarfs Mine Train roller coaster, in which the seven dwarfs sing their famous song "Heigh-Ho" in Mandarin for the first time, and Hunny Pot Spin, a teacup spin similar to Mad Hatter's Tea Party at Hong Kong Disneyland but with a honeypot design and the sound of humming bees from the locally popular *Winnie the Pooh* series. Alice is Disney's legacy project. In 1923, Walt Disney adapted one of his childhood favorite stories and produced the short film *Alice's Wonderland* combining live-action with animation. Years later in 1951,

Walt revived it as a full-length animated feature, *Alice in Wonderland*. In 1958, the Alice in Wonderland attraction debuted at Disneyland. To Walt Disney, "Disneyland is like Alice stepping through the Looking Glass" because stepping through the portals of Disneyland is like entering another world (Smith, 2001: 47). At Shanghai Disneyland, the legacy Alice attraction has a local twist. It is the first one in the world to feature new images of characters, such as the story's primary antagonist Red Queen, from Tim Burton's locally popular 2010 feature film *Alice in Wonderland*, which was released in China with a local box office exceeding US$30 million.

Another attraction based on a popular movie at Fantasyland is Frozen: A Sing-Along Celebration. *Frozen* (2013) is Disney's blockbuster animated feature, which reached about US$50 million at the box office in China. At Shanghai Disneyland, the majority of the guest-facing staff are local Chinese. Frozen: A Sing-Along Celebration is one of the few featuring Westerners to resonate with the audience's imagination. However, even Western faces have a local touch at Shanghai Disneyland. Here, actresses and actors with foreign faces all speak Mandarin (with a Western accent), which is another "distinctly Chinese" feature of Shanghai Disneyland. Interestingly, when the Western performer sang "let it go" in Mandarin on stage, the audience preferred singing the song in English because the Mandarin lyrics "*sui ta ba*," a direct translation of "let it go," sounded stranger than the English lyrics as my informants commented. Brannen (1992) argues that Tokyo Disneyland is recontextualized in two forms of making the exotic familiar and keeping the exotic exotic. In the case of the localization of the lyrics "let it go," when the encoder fails to make the exotic familiar, the decoder volunteers to keep the exotic exotic.

A major difference at Shanghai Disneyland's Fantasyland is the removal of Disney's iconic ride It's a Small World, an attraction first built by Walt Disney for the New York World Fair in 1964 and built again one year later at the first Disneyland in Anaheim. In Walt Disney's words, "Physically, Disneyland would be a small world in itself" (Smith, 2001: 48). This boat ride attraction features children of the world in miniature with uniform smiles and uniform Anglo-Saxon faces in different costumes repetitively singing "It's a Small World After All." It is a popular ride at Disneyland, including Hong Kong Disneyland. The absence of It's a Small World at Shanghai Disneyland serves to follow the Chinese partners' instruction to avoid a consistent worldwide Disneyland look and to circumvent the impression of cultural imperialism.

Adventure Isle

Walt Disney described the adventure-themed land as a place of "adventure, romance, and mystery" with "exotic flowers and eerie sounds of the jungle" (Smith, 2001: 63). At Shanghai Disneyland, the newly created adventure-themed land is Adventure Isle. This land was designed by a team with members from Asia, North America, and Europe. To help the team understand local culture, Walt Disney Imagineering hired local cultural consultants to share local cultural phenomena, including popular talent shows and documentaries such as *A Bite of China*.

Like at Disneyland Paris, the famous Jungle Cruise is absent from Adventure Isle at Shanghai Disneyland to avoid the notion of a colonial past and the imperialist mentality of the late 19th and early 20th centuries (Van Maanen, 1992). Replacing Jungle Cruise is Soarin' Over The Horizon (Soarin'), the first international version of the original Disneyland's Soarin' Over California. Soarin' is a virtual-tour ride "flying" around iconic landmarks, cities, and natural attractions of the world's six continents over the photography done with high-definition cameras, laser illumination, and proprietary shooting techniques. It features Matterhorn mountain in Switzerland, the Neuschwanstein castle in Bavaria, the Sydney Opera House in Australia, a balloon festival in Monument Valley in the American Southwest, the Iguazu waterfalls in Brazil, a deserted island in the South Pacific, the Eiffel Tower in Paris, the pyramids in Egypt, the Arctic Circle in Greenland, the Taj Mahal in India with a smell of roses, and a savanna in Africa. In order to increase local relevance, the Shanghai Disneyland version of Soarin' extends the American version to feature China's Great Wall and end on the host city Shanghai's skyline, including its landmark Oriental Pearl Tower, and a fireworks display across the sky of Pudong.

Another heavy dose of "distinctly Chinese" elements at Adventure Isle is the 30-minute stage show *Tarzan: Call of the Jungle* at Storyhouse Stage next to Soarin'. This show was developed and directed by a local Chinese female talent, Lee Xining, to retell Edgar Rice Burroughs' classic tale about an orphaned boy raised by apes in an African jungle. At Shanghai Disneyland, this show exhibits Chinese acrobatic stunts in the company of special visual effects and rock music. Leading characters Tarzan and Jane, as well as their animal friends, are all transformed to local acrobatics masters. Some audiences enjoy such a localization effort. An informant told me how her family appreciated the show by saying that it was worth the entrance admissions just to see this Tarzan show. However, some are not impressed. "Why are we here at Disneyland to see Chinese acrobatics that we don't even want to see in our hometown?" asked a father sitting next to me at the show. As Hall (1980: 125) argues, "decodings do not follow inevitably from encodings." Both dominant and oppositional readings were identified at this Tarzan show.

Also featured at Shanghai Disneyland's Adventure Isle are Roaring Rapids and Camp Discovery. Roaring Rapids is a river rafting ride that goes through Adventure Isle's highest peak, Roaring Mountain, with a newly created mysterious creature and eerie sounds. Camp Discovery provides a variety of expeditions to unravel the wonders of the island. Both attractions reflect Walt Disney's original concept of the adventure-themed land to encode adventure and mystery.

Tomorrowland

Walt Disney perceived Tomorrowland as "a vista into a world of wondrous ideas, signifying man's achievements... and the hope for a peaceful and unified world" (Smith, 2001: 68). At the original Disneyland built in 1955 in Anaheim, Walt's Tomorrowland represented the then future of the year 1986. For Shanghai Disneyland, the biggest challenge for the designers was how to tell the story of Tomorrowland in a city that "has been a world of the future," said Scot Drake, executive creative director of Tomorrowland for Shanghai Disneyland (Yang, 2015). The creative mandate of this themed land is stated as showcasing humanity, nature, and technology in perfect harmony, which echoes Walt Disney's original idea with an additional local stroke of harmony, one of the core values of "socialism with Chinese characteristics" the Chinese government promotes.

The most popular ride at the other Disneyland's Tomorrowland is the rollercoaster Space Mountain, which is absent at Shanghai Disneyland. Such exclusion serves to avoid reminding people of strong American nationalism and to increase the level of differences for the park. Replacing Space Mountain as Tomorrowland's anchor ride at Shanghai Disneyland is the world's first TRON Lightcycle Power Run (TRON) coaster ride. This ride is based on the *Tron* movies, although the 1982 movie *Tron* and its 2010 sequel *TRON: Legacy* are virtually unknown in China. TRON is one of Disney's fastest coasters, placing riders atop individual two-wheeled lightcycles launched into a space filled with lights and sound effects similar to the environment of Space Mountain. The track for TRON is 966 meters long. The cable and wiring required to run it is reported to be able to circle Shanghai 37 times. To directly convey the message of this ride, which travels 60 miles per hour, TRON Lightcycle Power Run is translated as "Superfast Light Cycle" in Chinese.

In addition to the pioneering TRON ride, like the other Disneyland, Shanghai Disneyland's Tomorrowland hosts attractions based on locally popular toon and film images, including the Buzz Lightyear Planet Rescue ride, Stitch Encounter, Baymax photo booth, and Star Wars Launch Bay, which feature a collection of props and set pieces from the *Star Wars* series, as well as walk-around Darth Vader and StormTroopers, iconic characters from the movie series.

Every Disneyland has a daily parade. The one at Shanghai Disneyland, known as Mickey's Storybook Express, running from Tomorrowland, around the Gardens of Imagination, and through Fantasyland, has the longest route among all Disneyland. This parade is led by Mickey Mouse with floats featuring dozens of Disney characters. The most discussed float in China is the Mulan float with dragon carvings. On the float, warrior Mulan in her male soldier disguise rides on the giant horse Kahn, as depicted in the 1998 animated feature *Mulan*. An informant told me how proud she was when seeing the Mulan float: "I was so touched. The horse was so tall. Mulan on it appeared so powerful. It is Disney's salute to our great nation of China."

Treasure Cove

At Shanghai Disneyland, it is not only attractions that are inspired by Disney's movies like *TRON* but also an entire themed land, Treasure Cove, inspired by the blockbuster movie franchise *Pirates of the Caribbean*. Treasure Cove is Disney's first pirate-themed land. This land features a full-sized pirate ship, a Caribbean style town, the world's first Pirates of the Caribbean: Battle for the Sunken Treasure ride, Explorer Canoes, and a Shipwreck Shore water play area. In order to drive the synergy effect, on May 11, 2017, Disney premiered *Pirates of the Caribbean: Dead Men Tell No Tales* movie at Shanghai Disney Resort with a party at Treasure Cove after the screening. It was the first time that China hosted the world premiere of a Disney movie.

Shanghai Disneyland is the largest Disneyland outside of the United States with innovation and cutting-edge technology that was not available in Disney's earlier parks. The best example of such technological advances is the boat ride Pirates of the Caribbean: Battle for the Sunken Treasure (Pirates), the largest attraction at Shanghai Disneyland, taking up 16,340 square meters. This high-tech version is different from the original Pirates of the Caribbean attraction, which opened at Disneyland Anaheim in 1967 overseen by Walt Disney. At Shanghai Disneyland, it

"Distinctly Chinese" representations of Shanghai Disneyland 75

is a heritage ride with the most advanced technology and a locally familiar movie character, Johnny Depp's Captain Jack Sparrow, to steal treasure from the movie's computer-generated image of Caption Davy Jones while meeting virtual monsters in a high-seas adventure.

Contrary to the high-tech ride of Pirates, Explorer Canoes is a people-powered ride inspired by the decades-long canoe rides at Disneyland in the United States and Tokyo Disneyland. At Shanghai Disneyland, the canoes paddle from Dead Man's Dock to travel around Treasure Cove's landmarks such as Skull Island and Lighthouse Ruins. Shipwreck Shore is a water play area where the audience can fire a cannon and visit a captain's quarters aboard Captain Gibbs' ship, the Siren's Revenge. Another first at Treasure Cove is *Eye of the Storm: Captain Jack's Stunt Spectacular*, a 30-minute stage show.

Walt Disney Grand Theater

Walt Disney Grand Theater in Shanghai Disneytown, part of Shanghai Disney Resort, hosted the world's first *The Lion King* stage show in Mandarin, which premiered on June 14, 2016 and was succeeded by the Mandarin version of *Beauty and the Beast* two years later. *The Lion King* Broadway show has been a success since its debut in 1997 and has reached 85 million people in about 22 countries as of 2016 when Shanghai Disneyland opened.

In this Chinese version, the main character young lion Simba's meerkat friend Timon in one scene, instead of dancing a Hula as in the original version, wears a Peking Opera costume and, with Simba's warthog friend Pumbaa, sings a theme song from the Cultural Revolution-era communist play *The Taking of Tiger Mountain*, which was made into a movie in 2014 and reached over US$140 million at the box office in China. Simba's evil uncle Scar sings a local modern hit, the so-called "divine tune," *Zui Xuan Minzu Feng* (the hottest ethnic style) from local pop duo Phoenix Legend. Furthermore, the movie's secondary antagonist hyenas speak fluent Mandarin with strong Northeast Chinese accents. (In the original version, Timon and Pumbaa speak English with a Brooklyn accent.) Curiously, the legendary Monkey King from the famous Chinese classic literature *Journey to the West* makes a special appearance to help Simba fight off the hyenas.

Disney tried hard, and maybe too hard, to act Chinese at this show. Unsurprisingly, this version of "The Lion King with Chinese characteristics" caused criticism from the local audience. Some said that their childhood memory was ruined, and some wondered why it was Northeast accent but not Shanghainese dialects to be featured.

However, it by all means pleased the government officials as it was an explicit example of how "Chinese elements highlight Shanghai Disneyland," a headline on China Central Television's website.

Dual-encoded "Distinctly Chinese" discourse

After visiting Shanghai Disneyland, some did not find the park "distinctly Chinese" and commented that the most Chinese element about Shanghai Disneyland was the visitors. However, under the discourse Disney created, being "distinctly Chinese" did not only refer to traditional Chinese culture. As Nancy Seruto, executive producer of Treasure Cove for Shanghai Disneyland, stated,

> "If you go into a foreign country with an openness that there is more than one right way to do things, then ultimately the product ends up being distinctly part of that culture."
>
> (Niles, 2016)

In July 2015, when the park design was almost finalized, Disney revealed Shanghai Disneyland as a Disney park filled with firsts. On the opening day, Disney further framed the themed lands at Shanghai Disneyland as a unique experience, imagined and created especially for China. Other than a Disney park of firsts, Disney's then chief executive officer Robert Iger called Shanghai Disneyland "the most technologically advanced (park) ever constructed by Disney" (Shanghai Daily, 2016). In other words, for Shanghai Disneyland, Disney rearranges the meaning of being "distinctly Chinese" which encodes both Chinese cultural references and contemporary Chinese preferences of uniqueness and technological advances (Table 5.1).

Table 5.1 Dual encodings of the "distinctly Chinese" discourse for Shanghai Disneyland

"Distinctly Chinese"	Signifier	Signified
Chinese cultural references	Chinese cuisines; symbols and language in themed lands, attractions, and entertainment performances.	The China Dream (the great rejuvenation of the Chinese nation)
Contemporary Chinese preferences	Uniqueness (China First) of themed lands and attractions. Technological advances of attractions.	

"Distinctly Chinese" representations of Shanghai Disneyland 77

Chinese cultural references suggest local symbols, local legends, local languages, and local cuisines. To some extent, Chinese cultural references celebrate the China Dream, or the great rejuvenation of the Chinese nation, proposed by President Xi Jinping. Contemporary Chinese preferences, the second layer of being "distinctly Chinese," encode uniqueness and technological advances. In addition to better engaging the local audience to maximize the profits, contemporary Chinese preferences of uniqueness (China First) and technological advances are also coherent with the China Dream thesis because, in Xi's idea, innovation is one of the core ways to spread the Chinese spirit and realize the China Dream.

Chinese cultural references

Every themed land at Shanghai Disneyland infuses various extents of Chinese cultural elements with the central area of the park showcasing the most intensified efforts. Gardens of Imagination in the center of Shanghai Disneyland is the themed land with the strongest Chinese culture references, including Garden of Twelve Friends which features the twelve Chinese zodiac signs, and Wandering Moon Teahouse in Chinese architecture style that serves traditional Chinese cuisines. Shanghai Disneyland's centerpiece castle Enchanted Storybook Castle at Fantasyland also highlights Chinese symbols, such as the golden topping of peony.

As a themed land stimulating consumption, the most Chinese encodings at the single entrance street, Mickey Avenue, are the product designs, such as Minnie Mouse in Chinese empress style and the Chinese cuisines in the Café. Adventure Isle, the themed land next to Mickey Avenue, showcases vivid local color as well: Soarin' Over The Horizon incorporates local images of the Great Wall and Shanghai landmarks; the 30-minute *Tarzan: Call of the Jungle* stage show exhibits Chinese acrobatics.

Treasure Cove and Tomorrowland, further away from the entrance on the side areas of the park, exhibit a lesser extent of Chinese cultural references. Treasure Cove presents Chinese signage and Chinese staff in pirate's costumes chatting with the audience in Mandarin. At Tomorrowland, in addition to the local signs and language, Chinese element is found in food: Sichuan chicken burgers at Stargazer Grill. At Shanghai Disneyland, Western cuisines are often seasoned with a Chinese taste, such as Mickey Mouse-shaped pizza topped with Peking duck. Fusion is also identified in Minnie Mouse red bean buns and meat mooncakes in the shape of Mickey Mouse.

Contemporary Chinese preferences

What local audiences expect to experience at Shanghai Disneyland is not necessarily traditional Chinese culture or Chinese food. "If we want to experience heavy Chinese elements like Peking Opera or Yue Opera, why don't we build a Peking Opera Park but build Disneyland?" asked a Chinese local consultant for Shanghai Disneyland (Ren, 2016). Sometimes, the local Chinese flavor a Western taste. For example, before the Shanghai Disneyland opening, Disney's then chief executive officer Robert Iger suggested not to sell Disneyland's famous turkey legs to China to minimize the foreignness of the park: "I thought (selling turkey legs) was a mistake, but we are selling 3,000 a day" (Shanghai Daily, 2016).

At Shanghai Disneyland, contemporary Chinese preferences, the second layer of being "distinctly Chinese," envision both uniqueness (China first) and technological advances. In terms of uniqueness, about 20 unique or "the first" features at Shanghai Disney Resort are identified: the first Steamboat Mickey fountain at the entrance; the first entrance street named Mickey Avenue; the first Gardens of Imagination; the first Gardens of Twelve Friends featuring the twelve Chinese zodiac signs; the first three-story restaurants in Chinese architecture style; the tallest, largest, most interactive Disneyland castle for the first time dedicated to all Disney princesses with multiple entrances; the first topping of the castle with a local flower; the first Mulan dining hall in the castle; the first Voyage to the Crystal Grotto to take the audience through the base of the castle; the first Alice in Wonderland Maze inspired by Tim Burton's 2010 movie; the first carousel ride themed to *Fantasia*; the seven dwarfs singing their famous song in Mandarin for the first time; the Roaring Mountain attraction with a newly created creature; the first international Soarin' Over attraction featuring China's Great Wall and the host city Shanghai's landmarks; the first Tarzan stage show with heavy Chinese acrobatics stunts; the first pirate-themed land Treasure Cove; the first Pirates of the Caribbean ride: Battle for the Sunken Treasure; the first TRON Lightcycle Power Run ride at Tomorrowland; the longest parade route of all Disneyland with a Mulan float; and the first *The Lion King* show in Mandarin.

Contemporary Chinese preferences also encode technological advances. Cultural conglomerates tend to regard imaginative innovation as the heart of wealth creation and social renewal (Hartley, 2005). Disney is notably famous for its "imagineering" of continuous exploration and experimenting to blend creative imagination with advanced technology. Among all Disneyland, Shanghai Disneyland features the largest percentage of new content with an emphasis on technology and a vision for the future to address modern China's aspiration to technological advances. At the Shanghai Disneyland's opening ceremony, highlighted by both Disney and the Chinese government was the word "innovation." Technoscape appears to have generated a promised land for Disney and its Chinese partner.

As a global cultural conglomerate, Disney's text is carefully coded (Wasko et al., 2001). There is not much discrepancy between Shanghai Disneyland's representations and the dual-encoded "distinctly Chinese" discourse Disney created. The dual encodings of the "distinctly Chinese" discourse that denotes both Chinese cultural references and contemporary Chinese preferences contributed to the park's positive business performance. In one year in June 2017, Shanghai Disneyland reached 11 million visitors, which exceeded Disney and its Chinese partner Shanghai Shendi Group's expectations.

Disneyland with Chinese characteristics

By joining the World Trade Organization in 2001, the reformed China found a place in the global capital, while striving to keep the contradictions between capital and people in suspension. In the process of transforming China to a Party publicity Inc. (He, 2000) that promotes the party image instead of brainwashing people, the Chinese party–state aims to exploit global capital economically and culturally, while continuing to play an essential role in regulating the media to take charge of the power battles. Through an examination of China's film policies from 1994 to 2012, Su (2014) argues a reversal of power relationship in international communication. The Chinese party–state reinforces its authority by negotiating foreign interest in the lucrative Chinese market while advancing its cultural industries to promote Chinese soft power.

Chinese Communist Party has been successfully reshaping popular culture to a socialist propaganda (Hung, 1996). All foreign content must serve China's interests to promote China's goals in an anti-imperialist way. In a study focusing on magazine publishing in Beijing, it was found that "the 'global' is no longer a dominating power, but a resourceful partner for flexible domestication" (Ma, 2013: 91). Even after the reform after joining the World Trade Organization, cultural content is required to ensure the socialist nature. Glocalization in China thus turns into the "nationalization of (global) culture" (Fung, 2008: 36)

The design of Disneyland is more flexible than previous studies on Disneyland concluded. As Walt Disney put it, "Disneyland is like a piece of clay, if there is something I don't like, I'm not stuck with it. I can reshape and revamp" (Smith, 2001: 53). Shanghai Disneyland is purposely constructed to be different from the other Disneyland as "China's Disneyland." Under the "distinctly Chinese" discourse Disney created for Shanghai Disneyland, the representations based on Chinese cultural references and contemporary Chinese preferences of uniqueness and technological advances are coherent with the Chinese party–state's China Dream thesis. Furthermore, at Shanghai Disneyland, every themed land that is also available at the other Disneyland excludes a signature name, such as Main Street USA, or iconic rides, such as It's a Small World, Jungle Cruise, and Space Mountain to minimize a universal appearance and avoid the impression of cultural imperialism.

Successful strategies are often bound by hegemonic order. This is particularly explicit in China where cultural enterprises tend to be subsumed into other developing policies. To minimize its potential threat to the Chinese party–state, a global cultural company needs to develop politically correct local strategies to avoid cultural or political sensitivity for a chance to thrive in this market. Consequently, Shanghai Disneyland is constructed as Disneyland with Chinese characteristics.

Unlike Hong Kong Disneyland, which adopts surface localization of local cuisines or Chinese Feng Shui, Shanghai Disneyland applies structural localization into the entire park design. In *The Disneyization of Society*, Bryman (2004) identifies two forms of localization: anticipatory localization and responsive localization. The former adapts to local conditions in anticipation of how they are likely to be received, and the latter is compelled to adapt as a result of the contact with local conditions. With an excessive emphasis on non-Western representations of anticipatory localization, Shanghai Disneyland is likely to induce responsive Westernization, instead of responsive localization, especially when the Chinese government increases its openness to global forces. An example is Toy Story Land, the first major expansion of Shanghai Disneyland. In this themed land, only surface localization, such as local language and cuisines, is observed.

The "authentically Disney and distinctly Chinese" representations of Shanghai Disneyland indicate an effort of glocalizaiton. Yet, both the exclusion to avoid the critics of cultural imperialism and the inclusion of Chinese cultural references and contemporary Chinese preferences suggest the predominance of the Chinese party–state in the production of Shanghai Disneyland. State-owned Shanghai Shendi Group, the majority shareholder of Shanghai Disneyland, was the final approver for the design of the park. In order to maximize the company's economic gains in lucrative China, Disney eagerly designed and constructed a unique, technologically advanced park, which promoted audience engagement and, more importantly, orchestrated with the Chinese party–state's political agenda. In other words, as with the ownership structure and the local identities of Shanghai Disneyland, the park's representations suggest *state-capital-led glocalization*: glocalization led by economic capital *of* the state and economic capital *with* the state.

Bibliography

Brannen, M. (1992). Bwana Mickey: Constructing cultural consumption at Tokyo Disneyland. In Tobin, J. (Ed.), *Re-Made in Japan*, 216–235. New Haven: Yale University Press.

Bryman, A. (2004). *The Disneyization of society*. London: SAGE Publications Ltd.

Clave, S.A. (2007). *The global theme park industry*. Oxfordshire: Cabi.

Davis, S. (1996). The theme park: Global industry and cultural form. *Media, Culture & Society*, 18, 399–422.

Eco, U. (1986). *Travels in hyper-reality*. London: Picador.

Fung, A. (2008). *Global capital, local culture: Transnational media corporations in China*. New York: Peter Lang.

Hall, S. (1980). Encoding/decoding. In Hall, S. et al. (Ed.), *Culture, media, language: Working papers in cultural studies, 1972–79*, 117–127. London: Hutchinson.

Hartley, J. (2005). *Creative industries*. Oxford: Blackwell Publishing.

He, Z. (2000). Working with a dying ideology: Dissonance and its reduction in Chinese Journalism. *Journalism Studies*, 1(4), 599–616.

Hewitt, D. (2016, June 16). Shanghai Disneyland to unleash incredible potential of Chinese market, company thinking of expanding Park: CEO Bob Iger. *International Business Times*. Retrieved January 20, 2020, from https://www.ibtimes.com/shanghai-disneyland-unleash-incredible-potential-chinese-market-company-thinking-2382270.

Hung, C.T. (1996). *War and popular culture: Resistance in modern China 1937–1945*. Berkeley and Los Angeles, CA: University of California Press.

Lukas, S.A. (2007). *The themed space: Locating culture, nation, and self*. New York: Lexington Books.

Ma, E. (2013). Saving face for magazine covers: New forms of transborder visuality in urban China. In Anthony, Y.H. Fung (Ed.), *Asian popular culture: The global (dis)continuity*, 76–93. New York: Routledge.

Niles, R. (2016, November 17). Legends 2016: How Disney built Shanghai Disneyland. *Theme Park Insider*. Retrieved January 20, 2020, from http://www.themeparkinsider.com/flume/201611/5339/.

Nunlist, T. (2016, December 15). Behind the scenes in the Magic Kingdom. *CKGSB Knowledge*. Retrieved January 20, 2020, from https://knowledge.ckgsb.edu.cn/2016/12/15/conversations/shanghai-disney-resort-behind-scenes/.

Ren, H.L. (2016, June 16). Disney's China dream (in Chinese). *Xinmin Weekly*, 24, 8–15.

Schultz, J. (1988). The fabulous presumption of Disney World: Magic Kingdom in the wilderness. *The Georgia Review*, 42, 275–312.

Shanghai Daily (2016, July 13). Disney chief claims a million people visited park. *Shanghai Daily*. Retrieved January 12, 2020, from https://www.sohu.com/a/104993670_161402.

Smith, D. (2001). *The quotable Walt Disney*. New York: Disney Editions.

Su, W. (2014). Cultural policy and film industry as negotiation of power: The Chinese State's role and strategies in its engagement with global Hollywood 1994–2012. *Pacific Affairs*, 87(1), 93–114.

Tan, W. (2015, November 13). Classic characters ready to welcome Disney guests. *Shanghai Daily*. Retrieved January 20, 2020, from http://www.shanghaidaily.com/feature/Classic-characters-ready-to-welcome-Disney-guests/shdaily.shtml.

Urry, J. (1995). *Consuming places*. London: Routledge.

Van Maanen, J. (1992). Displacing Disney: Some notes on the flow of culture. *Qualitative Sociology*, 15, 5–35.

Wasko, J., Phillips, M. & Meehan, E. (2001). *Dazzled by Disney: The global Disney audiences project*. London: Leicester University Press.

Yang, J. (2015, October 30). Disney team conjures up a 'new' tomorrowland. *Shanghai Daily*. Retrieved January 20, 2020, from https://archive.shine.cn/feature/Disney-team-conjures-up-a-new-Tomorrowland/shdaily.shtml.

Yoshimoto, M. (1994). Images of empire: Tokyo Disneyland and Japanese cultural imperialism. In Smoodin, E. (Ed.), *Disney discourse: Producing the Magic Kingdom*, 181–199. New York: Routledge.

Zukin, S. (1991). *Landscapes of power: From Detroit to Disney World*. Oakland: University of Calilfornia Press.

6 Implications of the differences of Shanghai Disneyland

Previous studies tend to link Disney with cultural imperialism. Being one of the world's largest entertainment companies, Disney is often criticized as a cultural imperialist that promotes the imperialist ideology with an exercise of exploitative control over resources and people's values through economic dominance. China, a country with a strong awareness of its historical greatness, is sensitive about any imperialist attempt. In order to avoid being called a cultural imperialist for a chance to survive and thrive in the lucrative Chinese market, Disney carefully builds Shanghai Disneyland as Disneyland with Chinese characteristics.

Beyond cultural imperialism

Focusing on the production of Shanghai Disneyland, this book examines *production*'s relationships with *state*, *market*, park *identity*, and park *representation* (Figure 6.1). Here, identity refers to how Shanghai Disneyland sees itself and wishes to be seen with politics to advance the company's interests. Representation refers to the arrangement of the themed lands, inclusion and exclusion of attractions, and content of entertainment performances at Shanghai Disneyland. Strategy, in its business sense, refers to a set of guiding principles for a company to prioritize resources for the achievement of desired goals.

Production and state: Ownership structure of Shanghai Disneyland

Disney's production of Shanghai Disneyland is largely shaped by the Chinese party–state's regulations and political agenda. Shanghai Disneyland is a joint venture between The Walt Disney Company and the state-owned Shanghai Shendi Group. This joint venture has two owner companies and one management company. The management

84 *Implications of the differences of Shanghai Disneyland*

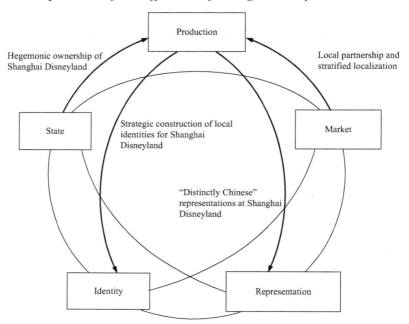

Figure 6.1 Production's relationships with state, market, park identity, and park representation in the case of Shanghai Disneyland

company is responsible for designing and operating the park on behalf of the owner companies.

According to China's *Catalogue for the Guidance of Foreign Investment Industries*, the construction of theme parks is one of the restricted investments, which are required to follow the Sino–foreign joint-venture only rule and the majority Chinese ownership rule. Accordingly, Disney forms a joint venture with the state-owned Shanghai Shendi Group and holds the minority of 43 percent shares in the owner companies. Although management of theme parks falls under the encouraged category without any joint-venture rule, Disney does not own 100 percent in the management company of Shanghai Disneyland. This is the first-ever special arrangement for Disney to engage the local in the management of Disneyland in which the company holds shares. For Disneyland Paris and Hong Kong Disneyland, Disney takes full charge of the management. The Chinese government allowed Disney to hold 70 percent of the shares in the management company in exchange for Disney's extensive sharing of its theme park expertise to promote the country's development goals of advancing the local tourism industry.

Based on consent rather than coercion, hegemony is maintained through ongoing articulation of opposing interests into the political affiliations of the hegemonic group. In the case of Shanghai Disneyland, the Chinese state utilizes its economic capital and enormous market size to accumulate both its economic capital through park revenues and its cultural capital of theme park management through the co-operation with Disney. On the other hand, Disney exchanges its cultural capital of theme park design and management for an opportunity to accumulate its economic capital in the Chinese market.

Major foreign cultural companies are cultivated to orchestrate with the party–state's agenda in China. Disney has a dedicated Department of Government Affairs in China to deliver targeted advocacy in support of business goals. On top of the strategies for the other Disneyland, such as synergy and recycling of old materials, in China, maintaining valuable government relations is Disney's main strategy. There will be no business in which to exercise any strategy if the Chinese party–state blocks or suspends Disney's practices, which is not uncommon in China. Denial of access to the lucrative Chinese market is the Chinese party–state's highhanded measure to force global capitals to comply with the government's interests.

Production and identity: Construction of local identities for Shanghai Disneyland

As an institutional tactic, identity embodies politics to address issues of access in order to protect and advance certain interests (Brantlinger, 1990; Turner, 2002). Unlike the other Disneyland outside of the United States, Disney constructed local identities for Shanghai Disneyland as "China's Disneyland" and "a citizen of Shanghai" for better audience engagement and, more importantly, to avoid social critics of cultural imperialism for better government relations.

Similar to the local identities for Shanghai Disneyland, Disney constructed a local image for the other lines of business in China. Back in 2005, Disney coined The Walt Disney Company (China) Ltd. as "The Chinese Walt Disney Company." In order to be "The Chinese Walt Disney Company," one important strategy is localization through local partnership and stratified localization. Under China's strong national protectionism and strict media policy, local partnership helps Disney with more cobranded products that are likely to qualify as local productions with better distribution opportunities in the market. Moreover, diversity exists within cultures. Stratified localization attending to various local tastes in different city tiers in populous China increases Disney's brand awareness and brand affinity to maximize the profit potential for the company.

Capitalism thrives on heterogeneity. Major global cultural companies increasingly tailor their products to differentiated global markets because embracing the differences in the local sites helps to sustain their business. In China, localization of global cultural products not only promotes audience engagement for a global cultural company to thrive in various city tiers but also enhances government relations to survive in the market. In order to demonstrate the company's commitment to the Chinese government, Disney constructed local images of "China's Disneyland" for Shanghai Disneyland and "The Chinese Walt Disney Company" for The Walt Disney Company (China) Ltd.

Production and representation: "Distinctly Chinese" representations of Shanghai Disneyland

Themed lands, attractions, and entertainment performances at Shanghai Disneyland are "authentically Disney and distinctly Chinese" as instructed by Robert Iger, former chief executive officer of The Walt Disney Company. All foreign content in China is supposed to serve China's interests to promote China's goals in an anti-imperialist way. The exclusion of iconic Disneyland rides from Shanghai Disneyland displays Disney's efforts to avoid the impression of cultural imperialism. Here, everything exotic must have a local twist. For example, the tallest Shanghai Disneyland castle is topped with a Chinese flower, Western performers speak Mandarin, and brand-new attractions with advanced technology are framed as created uniquely for China.

Connotations involve the symbolic, historic, and emotional matters connected to it (Peirce, 1991). For Shanghai Disneyland, Disney created a discourse to rearrange the meaning of being "distinctly Chinese," which denotes both Chinese cultural references and contemporary Chinese preferences of uniqueness (China First) and technological advances. Shanghai Disneyland was promoted as the most technologically advanced park ever constructed by Disney. It was also described as a Disney park filled with firsts. For example, the first Treasure Cove themed land, the first Disneyland castle for all princesses, and the first Gardens of Twelve Friends featuring the twelve Chinese zodiac signs. Shanghai Disneyland's representations under the "distinctly Chinese" discourse that encodes both Chinese cultural references and contemporary Chinese preferences are coherent with the China Dream thesis proposed by Chinese President Xi Jinping.

All in all, due to China's regulations on foreign investments, Disney owns the minority of 43 percent, while its Chinese partner owns the majority of 57 percent of Shanghai Disneyland. As China accumulates its economic capital, the state is getting more powerful in asserting its demands by pressurizing foreign cultural companies to share storytelling and technological advances to promote the country's development goals. The capitalist mode appears to have been divorced from its historical origin in the West. Non-Western countries are gradually empowered by economic prosperity with new self-confidence, which implies shifting or destruction of centers. Empowered by the state's economic capital and market size, China is realizing its China Dream and transforming the traditional central–peripheral roles in the discussion of cultural imperialism. Shanghai Disneyland was purposely created to be different from the other Disneyland to not only avoid the impression of cultural imperialism but also orchestrate with the Chinese political agenda.

State-capital-led Glocalization

For Tokyo Disneyland, a Japanese imagination of the American park, Raz argues that "the 'imperialist' here is the (Japanese) consumer rather than the (Western) producers" (Raz, 1999: 153). I am not taking such an extreme stand, but, rather, arguing the production of Shanghai Disneyland as an example of glocalization for a couple of reasons. First, unlike Tokyo Disneyland, of which Disney owns zero percent, 43 percent of the Shanghai Disneyland owner companies and 70 percent of the management company are Disney owned. Such ownership arrangements indicate that Disney plays by the Chinese party–state's rules, while retaining certain creative control in the making of Shanghai Disneyland. Second, the creative goal of being "authentically Disney and distinctly Chinese" suggests a Chinese Disneyland story elaborated in a Disney way to meet the Chinese partner's expectations. In other words, the park's representations of the themed lands, attractions, and entertainment performances are designed by Disney and approved by the Chinese partner, not solely created by the local like Tokyo Disneyland.

Although the production of Shanghai Disneyland indicates glocalization, not reverse imperialism as Raz (1999) implies of Tokyo Disneyland, its ownership structure, local identities, and a discourse of the "distinctly Chinese" representations disclose the predominance of the Chinese economic capital in the glocalization of Shanghai Disneyland. In other words, it is *state-capital-led glocalization* in the case of Shanghai Disneyland.

88 *Implications of the differences of Shanghai Disneyland*

State-capital-led glocalization encodes two meanings (Figure 6.2). First, it indicates glocalization led by economic capital *of* the state, that is, the state's direct economic investment. Shanghai Disneyland is state-capital-led because, in the owner companies, the Chinese state-owned Shanghai Shendi Group holds the majority 57 percent of the shares. According to Disney's annual financial report, the investment in Shanghai Disneyland is funded in accordance with each shareholder's ownership percentage. That is, the majority of the park's economic capital came from the Chinese party–state. Second, state-capital-led glocalization suggests glocalization led by economic capital *with* the state, that is, the market potential. In China, global players need to meet the state agenda prior to the market interests. For the tremendous Chinese market potential, a global cultural company is willing to compromise and share its cultural production expertise in exchange for potential economic returns, as revealed in the negotiation and production of Shanghai Disneyland. For Disney, pursuing maximum returns on the investment is the company's top priority.

State-capital-led glocalization is generalizable to the other global cultural products in China and in the other countries with tremendous market potential, for example, Universal Studios Beijing. Like Shanghai Disneyland, this project is a lesson in patience for the global player, Comcast NBC Universal. Universal Studios Beijing took 13 years in negotiation. It was approved by China's National Development and Reform Commission in September 2014, broke ground in October 2016, and was scheduled to open in 2021. In terms of the ownership structure, like Shanghai Disneyland, Universal Studios Beijing is regulated by the joint-venture only rule and the majority Chinese

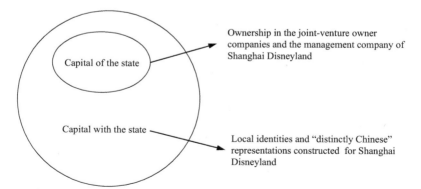

Figure 6.2 Dual encodings of "state-capital" in the concept of *state-capital-led glocalization* and respective outputs in the case of Shanghai Disneyland

ownership rule. The US$8 billion project of Universal Studios Beijing is jointly owned and operated by state-owned Beijing Shouhuan Cultural Tourism Investment Co., Ltd. and Comcast NBC Universal. Comcast NBC Universal owns 70 percent in the management company and 30 percent in the construction company of Universal Studios Beijing.

With regard to the park representations, Universal Studios Beijing will be the largest among all six Universal Studios in the world. In order to pay homage to the Chinese culture, Universal Studios Beijing announced its plan to offer China-themed attractions, in addition to locally well-known ones when the project was approved. In October 2019, Universal Studios Beijing revealed its park layout of seven themed lands: Kung Fu Panda Land of Awesomeness, Transformers: Metrobase, Minion Land, The Wizarding World of Harry Potter, Jurassic World Isla Nublar, Hollywood, and WaterWorld. Among them, Kung Fu Panda Land, which encodes Chinese cultural relevance, was highlighted.

Similar to Shanghai Disneyland, the production of Universal Studios Beijing is state-capital-led glocalization, which is led by both economic capital of the state and economic capital with the state. Like Disney, in order to pursue the maximum returns in the Chinese market, Comcast NBC Universal is willing to make compromises as a minority ownership holder, share its global theme park management expertise with its local partner, and create locally relevant representations.

State-capital-led glocalization is also likely generalizable to the other countries. In a lucrative market which owns abundant economic capital of the state and economic capital with the state, a global company is proven willing to make compromises and follow the majority local ownership rule in exchange for the potential returns on its investment as the production of Shanghai Disneyland shows. In other words, we see more flexibility in the capital formation of a cultural entity nowadays.

The infusion of state-capital in a cultural entity, as in the case of Shanghai Disneyland, suggests a call for the political economy approach to examine the complexity of the interlock of the political inference and the economic ownership in a cultural entity. From the perspective of political economy of communication, assuming that the media or the cultural entities are private-owned, there are political and economic constraints on these entities. The approach of political economy examines these constraints and how the owners of the cultural entities survive these constraints. Lee (2001) summarizes two approaches to the political economy of the media: the liberal–pluralist approach and the

90 *Implications of the differences of Shanghai Disneyland*

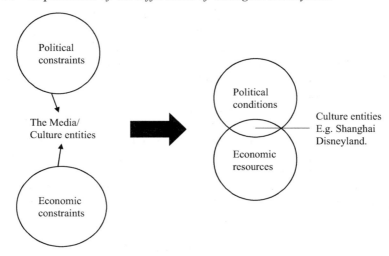

Figure 6.3 The approach of political economy of communication and Shanghai Disneyland

radical–Marxist approach. The former ("political" political economy) explains Third World developing countries, in which the state plays the primary role, and the latter ("economic" political economy) examines advanced capitalist countries, in which the role of the state is derived and capital accumulation is celebrated. In both approaches, assuming that the media are privately capitalized, the state either shapes or is subservient to the media to maximize the interests of the state. However, in the case of Shanghai Disneyland, which is mainly state capitalized, the state is not independent from a cultural entity as previous approaches to the political economy of communication suggest.

The production of Shanghai Disneyland indicates that political conditions, cultural entities, and economic resources are not totally separated (Figure 6.3). China has learned to capitalize on the market forces. It is not in the Chinese state's interest to suppress the global cultural entities through brutal cultural policies or authoritarian orders. Rather, it is the collaboration with global players, through which the local cultural industries could be further advanced, which the state would like to pursue.

Typology of glocalization

Drawing on the literature of various concepts about cultural globalization, state-capital-led glocalization appears opposite to cultural imperialism in terms of the local–global power play. It falls under the

Implications of the differences of Shanghai Disneyland 91

broad concept of transculturation, which refers to the process by which a culture is transformed by another before or during synthesis (Chan, 2002), and another broad concept of cultural hybridization which refers to "the ways in which forms become separated from existing practices and recombine with new forms in new practices" (Rowe & Schelling, 1991: 161). Along the axis of the global–local power relations, between cultural imperialism and state-capital-led glocalization, there are concepts like cultural appropriation which refers to an active process of unauthorized exclusive possession of symbols, artifacts, or technologies by members of another culture (Rogers, 2006), and Robertson's glocalization.

Robertson's idea of glocalization (1992) suggests a process of a global formation of locality when the local meets the global. Based on the migration strategies of Scottish football fans in North America, Giulianotti and Robertson (2007) proposed four forms of glocalization from the audience's perspective. The four forms are: relativization, accommodation, hybridization, and transformation. Relativization is one way to preserve the social actors' prior cultural practices within a new frame, in order to be distinctly different from the host culture; accommodation describes how social actors practically absorb the meanings associated with the host culture, in order to maintain key essence of the prior local culture; hybridization indicates how the host culture and the prior culture are synthesized to produce hybrid cultural practices; and transformation refers to how social actors come to favor the meanings associated with the host culture.

The above four forms of glocalization were based on an audience analysis. The finding of state-capital-led glocalization in the production of Shanghai Disneyland demands a discussion of the academic neglect of the typology of glocalization from the production perspective. As discussed in the previous section, state-capital-led glocalization is defined as glocalization led by both economic capital of the state (state's investments) and economic capital with the state (market potential). Based on these two kinds of capital, four categories of glocalization are identified as the state interference intensifies: capital-led glocalization, capital- and state-led glocalization, state-capital-led glocalization, and state-led glocalization (Figure 6.4).

Capital-led glocalization refers to glocalization led by economic capital with the state without any economic capital of the state. Capital-led glocalization is purely market-driven in a liberal political entity without strict regulations on the cultural products. Depending on the local market preference, the consequences of capital-led glocalization could be either global or local representations.

92 Implications of the differences of Shanghai Disneyland

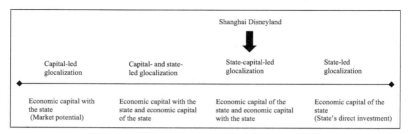

Figure 6.4 Four categories of glocalization

Two examples are Tokyo Disneyland and Disneyland Paris. Tokyo Disneyland is fully owned and operated by a local Japanese company, Oriental Land Co., Ltd. Under a format licensing deal, Disney shared 10 percent of the admission, 5 percent of food and merchandise, and 10 percent of corporate sponsorship (Wasko, 1996). In terms of the park representations, Tokyo Disneyland was designed as Americanized Disneyland in order to meet the market expectations. The local owner refused Disney's proposal of a Samurai Land or the Little Peach Boy Ride based on the local legends because the local Japanese did not want a Japanese version of Disneyland but preferred real Disneyland with an original American look for a foreign vacation in town (Brannen, 1992; Raz, 1999).

While at Disneyland Paris, which is owned by Disney and several investors without any state capital, upon the local audience's requests, Disney started to offer French wine although alcohol was originally a taboo at sanitized Disneyland. Also, the themed land Tomorrowland was replaced by Discoveryland because market research showed that the Europeans held skeptical attitude toward the wonders of science and technology (Van Maanen, 1992).

Capital- and state-led glocalization refers to glocalization led by economic capital with the state and economic capital of the state, with the former as the main driving force. That is, although both market and political gains are considered, the market is prior to the political agenda in this category of glocalization. Similar to capital-led glocalization, the consequences of capital- and state-led gloclaization could be an emphasis on the global or on the local.

For example, Hong Kong Disneyland. It is owned and operated by a joint venture company, the Hong Kong International Theme Parks Limited, with two shareholders: The Walt Disney Company and the Government of the Hong Kong Special Administration Region (HKSRG). Although the HKSRG owns 53 percent of Hong Kong Disneyland, Hong Kong Disneyland is designed to meet the audience's expectations in a liberal market for wholesome family entertainment, under the banner of promoting the political agenda of the HKSAR to develop Hong Kong as Asia's World City. Unlike Shanghai Disneyland, which is carefully framed as China's Disneyland, Hong Kong Disneyland does not have a distinct local identity. In terms of the park's representations, Hong Kong Disneyland is a replica of the original Disneyland in California, without placing an emphasis on the local because audiences in Hong Kong, the most Westernized city in China, are equipped with enough cultural capital to comprehend and resonate with the foreign concept of Disneyland.

State-capital-led glocalization, as discussed, refers to glocalization led by economic capital of the state and economic capital with the state. The cultural products are mainly state capitalized as Shanghai Disneyland illustrates. Both political and economic gains are considered, while the former is on top of the latter. As a consequence, the representations are largely local or framed as local like the "distinctly Chinese" discourse indicates.

State-led glocalization refers to glocalization led by the economic capital of the state. The cultural products under state-led glocalization are fully state-owned. It is the political gains, rather than the market profits, which the state would like to pursue through such investment. Under the state's supervision, the consequence of state-led glocalization is an emphasis on the local.

An example is Beijing 798 Art District, the site of the state-owned factories located in the Dashanzi area. Starting from 2002, these factories, such as Factory 798, which used to produce electronics, started to be developed to art galleries and design companies. Developing the cultural industries is a tool for branding Chinese cities (Fung, 2016). Beijing 798 Art District has been branded first unofficially by grass-roots artists to preserve the industrial area, and then officially to promote Beijing as a global city by appropriating the Western concept of the art districts, hosting international art exhibitions, and nurturing both local and foreign artists. Artistic activities in the 798 Art District are filtered by the Chinese government to minimize the risk of jeopardizing the state's interests and to promote an image of political harmony and open economy.

All in all, the four categories of glocalization of different conditions, considerations, and consequences (Table 6.1) illustrate various global–local dynamics in the process of a global formation of locality when the local meets the global.

In terms of the elements analyzed in this study of Shanghai Disneyland, the formation of the ownership in the owner companies

Table 6.1 Four categories of glocalization

	Capital-led	Capital- and state-led	State-capital-led	State-led
Condition	Capital with the state	Capital with the state and capital of the state	Capital of the state and capital with the state	Capital of the state
Consideration	Economic	Economic and political	Political and economic	Political
Consequence	An emphasis on the global or the local, depending on market preference	An emphasis on the global or the local, depending on market preference	An emphasis on the local	An emphasis on the local
Example	Tokyo Disneyland	Hong Kong Disneyland	Shanghai Disneyland	Beijing 798 Art District

of Shanghai Disneyland, in which China holds 57 percent, is the closest to state-led glocalization. The construction of local identities of "China's Disneyland" and "authentically Disney and distinctly Chinese" come next as a 50–50 glocal hybrid, followed by the formation of China's 30 percent ownership in the management company of Shanghai Disneyland. The closest to capital-led glocalization is the production of the Disney-designed park representation of which 80 percent is claimed to be "distinctly Chinese," but only about 20 percent of this 80 percent refers to traditional Chinese culture; the rest address contemporary Chinese preferences, which are framed by Disney as uniqueness (China First) and technological advances.

Such distances from state-led and capital-led glocalization indicate that, when economic capital is abundant, the more lacking in cultural capital an entity is, the further away it is from the state control. The management and representations of Shanghai Disneyland are further away from the state control because they require substantial cultural capital, which the Chinese state has not yet raised. The Chinese state is abundant in economic capital but lacking in cultural capital. As a result, China permitted Disney to own 70 percent in the management company of Shanghai Disneyland in order to accumulate the state's cultural capital when Disney shares its world-class theme park management expertise.

Contrary to the traditional critics of cultural imperialism on Disney, the study of Shanghai Disneyland finds that it is glocalization that best serves both the state and a global cultural company's interests. When the global meets the local, it is not imperialism but glocalization, in which the global and the local thrive together, that helps a global cultural product to thrive in a local market, or a local cultural artifact to prosper in a global market.

Bibliography

Brannen, M. (1992). Bwana Mickey: Constructing cultural consumption at Tokyo Disneyland. In Tobin, J. (Ed.), *Re-Made in Japan*, 216–235. New Haven: Yale University Press.

Brantlinger, P. (1990). *Crusoe's footprints: Cultural studies in Britain and America*. New York: Routledge.

Chan, J. (2002). Disneyfying and globalizing a Chinese legend Hua Mulan: A study of transculturation. In Chan, J. & McIntyre, B. (Ed.), *In search of boundaries: Communication, nation-state and cultural identities*, 225–248. Westport, CT: Ablex.

Fung, A. (2016). Strategizing for creative industries in China: Contradictions and tension in nation branding. *International Journal of Communication*, 10, 3004–3021.

Giulianotti, R., & Robertson, R. (2007). Forms of glocalization: Globalization and the migration strategies of Scottish football fans in North America. *Sociology*, 4(1), 133–152.

Lee, C.C. (2001). Rethinking political economy: Implications for media and democracy in Greater China. *Javnost - The Public*, 8(4), 81–102.

Peirce, C. (1991). *Peirce on signs: Writings on semiotic*. Chapel Hill, NC: The University of North Carolina Press.

Raz, R. (1999). *Riding the black ship: Japan and Tokyo Disneyland*. Cambridge: Harvard University Asia Center.

Robertson, R. (1992). *Globalization: Social theory and global culture*. London: SAGE Publications Ltd.

Rogers, R. (2006). From cultural exchange to transculturation: A review and reconceptualization of cultural appropriation. *Communication Theory*, 16, 474–503.

Rowe, W. & Schelling, V. (1991). *Memory and modernity: Popular cultures in Latin America*. London: Verso.

Turner, G. (2002). *British cultural studies*. London: Routledge.

Wasko, J. (1996). Understanding the Disney Universe. In Curran, J. & Gurevitch, M. (Ed.), *Mass media and society*, 348–365. New York: Arnold.

Van Maanen, J. (1992). Displacing Disney: Some notes on the flow of culture. *Qualitative Sociology*, 15, 5–35.

Index

A Bite of China 72
access 3–4, 10, 40, 60, 85
accommodation 41, 91
acquisition 14–15
adaptation 43
Adventure Isle 65–66, 72–73
Adventureland 19, 35, 46
affluent household 34, 58
Africa 72
African American 10
Akio, Morita 41
Aladdin 13, 68, 70
Alibaba Group Holding Ltd. 38
Alice Comedies 8
Alice in Wonderland 70–71, 78
American Broadcasting Company (ABC) 10–11, 13–14
American Chamber of Commerce, The 37
American nationalism 20, 66, 73
Anaheim (Disneyland): identity 46; opening 2, 11, 35; representation 20, 69–74
annual financial report 25, 30, 54, 88
anticipatory localization 80
Apple Daily 48
architecture 49, 60, 69, 77–78
Arctic Circle 72
As the Bell Rings 54
Asia's World City 19, 26, 93
aspiration 40, 47, 79
Astro Boy 53
Australia 72
autonomy 19, 40
Autumn Festival 18, 57

Bambi 9, 68
ban 16, 32, 53
Bass brothers 12
Baymax 55, 74
Beauty and the Beast 13, 70, 75
Beijing 798 Art District 93–94
Beijing Animation Center 36
Beijing Chung Kong Graduate School of Business 18
Beijing Neiliansheng 57
Beijing Shouhuan Cultural Tourism Investment Co. Ltd. 34, 89
BesTV 54
Big Hero Six 55
bilateral relation 24, 39
blockbuster 13, 51, 74
board member 14, 16, 25, 31, 33
Bourdieu, P. 50
box office 12–13, 38, 51, 55, 71, 75
brand affinity 2, 31, 37, 61, 86
brand awareness 2, 31, 37, 61, 86
Brannen, M. 46, 71, 92
Brave 70
Brazil 72
Britain 18, 20
Broadway 13, 75
Brooklyn 75
Bryman, A. 12, 42, 56, 80
Bund, the 21
Burroughs, Edgar Rice 72
Burton, Tim 71, 78
business segment 3, 15

cable network 14
Capital Cities/ABC Inc. 13

Index 97

capital- and state-led glocalization 92–94
capital-led glocalization 91–92, 94
capitalism 6, 42, 61, 86
capitalist mode 40, 87
Captain America 34, 68
Captain America: Civil War 55
Captain Davy Jones 75
Captain Jack Sparrow 75
carousel 68, 78
cast member 48
castle: Hong Kong Disneyland 17, 69; Neuschwanstein, Bavaria 72; Shanghai Disneyland 23, 51, 56, 69–70, 72, 77–78, 86; Shijingshan 35; Tokyo Disneyland 69
celebration 13, 23, 26, 51, 58, 69–71
celebrity 11, 51, 55
central–peripheral roles 5, 40, 87
chairman 11–12, 14–15, 28, 32, 34, 39, 57
Chairman Mao 37
challenge 14, 23, 37, 57
Chan, Anson 30
Chapek, Bob 15
Cheng, Fang 32
Chengdu (Sichuan province) 17, 57
Cheung, Stanley 15–17, 25, 52–54
chief executive officer (CEO): Chapek 15; Eisner 14, 16, 37–38; Iger 14–16, 20, 22–23, 32–33, 37–39, 41, 45, 49–50, 76, 78, 86
chief operating officer 14
child labor 57
Chimelong Ocean Kingdom 35
China Central Television (CCTV) 16, 34, 39, 53–54, 66, 76
China Central Television's Movie Channel (CCTV6) 1–2
China Dream 6, 39, 76–77, 80, 86–87
China Film Group 55
China Internet Network Development Report 38
China Internet Network Information Center 38
China Youth Daily 24
China's *Catalogue for the Guidance of Foreign Investment Industries* 4, 31, 33, 84

China's Ministry of Commerce 31
China's National Development and Reform Commission 31, 34, 88
China's National Enterprise Credit Information Publicity System 17, 28
China's Special Economic Zone 21
China's Wall Street 21
Chinese bureaucratic characteristics 41
Chinese Communist Party (CCP) 16, 18, 21, 32, 37, 40, 56, 79
Chinese Communist Youth League 24
Chinese cultural reference 6, 76–80, 86
Chinese Feng Shui 20, 50, 66, 80
Chinese New Year 39, 48, 57, 70
Chinese People's Political Consultative Committee 49
Chinese Princess Snow White 15
Chinese State Council 21
Chinese University of Hong Kong 25
'Chinese Walt Disney Company, The' 6, 8, 15–18, 52–58, 60, 86
Chinese zodiac 57, 67, 69, 77–78, 86
Ching Dynasty 57
Cinderella 10, 35, 69
circuit of culture 4
citizen of Shanghai 6, 45–46, 51, 60, 85
city tier 17, 57–58, 61, 86
Coca Cola 60
colonialism 18
colonization 59
Colony Theater (New York) 9
Columbia Broadcasting System (CBS) 11
Comcast (NBC Universal) 14, 33–34, 88–89
common family 34
competitor 14, 25–26, 35, 42
complement 25–26, 42
compliance 56
compromise 6, 36–38, 88–89
conflict 34, 42, 48
conglomerate 15, 41, 53, 78–79

98 *Index*

connotation 59, 66, 86
consequence 2, 7, 91–94
consumer product 3, 9, 15, 17, 32, 56–60
consumption 4, 25, 40, 59, 67, 77
contemporary Chinese preference 76–80, 86
context 2, 30, 38, 40, 45, 52, 65
Convention for the Extension of Hong Kong Territory 18
cooperation 24, 33, 46, 48, 55
Coppola, Francis 13
corporate enclosure of culture 3
corporate raider 12
counter flow 39–40
creative direction 3, 22–23, 45, 65
Creative Power Entertaining Corporation 14
crisis 33, 37, 43
critical distance 3
critical syncretism 60
criticism 56, 75
Crouching Tiger, Hidden Dragon 51
cuisine 20, 58, 68, 76–80
cultural appropriation 91
cultural capital 33, 36, 41–42, 85, 93
'cultural Chernobyl' 43, 47
cultural flow 40
cultural hybridization 91
cultural industries 18, 36, 79, 93
Cultural Revolution 16, 75

Dalai Lama 37
Dalian Wanda Group 34–35, 49
Darth Vader 74
Davos (2017) 33
debut 2, 11, 71
decoding 51, 71, 73, 81
dedication 23, 46–50
Deng, Xiaoping 19, 57
Department of Army and Navy
Department of Treasury, Agriculture and State 10
dependency theory 59
Depp, Johnny 75
Depression, the 9
descriptive examination 6
destruction 40, 87
Dick Tracy 13

digital connection 18, 52, 54
discourse 6, 59, 76–80, 86–87, 93
Discoveryland 92
Disney Channel 2, 12, 14, 36–39, 49, 54
Disney Direct-to-Consumer and International 3, 15
Disney English Learning Center 17, 57
Disney International Labor Standards (ILS) 56
Disney Internet 16
Disney Junior 39
Disney Media Networks 3, 15
Disney MGM Studios 13
Disney on Ice 16
Disney Parks and Resorts 2, 15
Disney Parks, Experiences and Products 3, 15
Disney Plus 15
Disney Princess 17, 69–70, 78, 86
Disney, Roy 8, 11–12, 14
Disney Store 13, 52–53
Disney Studio Entertainment 3, 12, 15, 54–56
Disney, Walt 3, 8–13, 37, 47–48, 60, 68–74, 80
Disneyfication 1, 56, 60
Disneyization 56, 80
Disneyization of Society, The 80
Disneyland 10
Disneyland Incorporated 10
Disneyland Paris: glocalization 43, 92; identity 46–50; opening 2, 13, 17, 19, 50; ownership 28–29, 31, 33, 84; representation 60, 66, 69, 72
DisneyLife 37–38
Disneyness 11
Disney's Animal Kingdom 13
Disney's California Adventure 13
Disney's Code of Conduct 57
Disney's Department of Government Affairs 38–39, 85
Disney's healthy food guidelines 1–2
Disney's production guidelines 1–2
Disney's standards and practices 1
Disney's Wonderful World of Color 11

Disneytown 65–66, 75
diversity 42, 57, 59, 61, 85
'divine tune' 75
document analysis 3
dominance 59–60, 83
dominant reading 73
Donald Duck 15, 49
Dragon Boat Festival 57
Dragon Club 16, 53
Dragon TV 51
Dreaming Man, The 55
DreamWorks 14
Dumbo 9, 68

Egypt 72
Eiffel Tower 72
Eight Immortals 16
Eisner, Michael 12–14, 16, 37–38
empire 1, 6, 14, 18, 59
employment agreement 4
encoding 73, 76–79, 88
engagement 18, 50, 52, 60, 81, 85–86
entrance admission 22, 24, 40, 72, 92
ESPN 54
Euro Disneyland *see* Disneyland Paris
exclusion 6, 65–76, 83, 86–87
Eye of the Storm: Captain Jack's Stunt Spectacular 75

Fan, Xiping 28, 31, 32
Fantasia 9, 68, 70, 78
Fantasyland 19, 35, 46, 58, 65–71, 74, 77
film revenue-sharing system 16, 54
Finding Nemo 13
firework 70, 72
fiscal year 2, 25, 29–30, 34
Flaming Mountain 16
Florida 2, 11, 13, 24, 26
foreignness 46, 78
franchise 14, 74
Frank School 59
Frozen 51, 58, 70–71
Fung, A. 2–3, 30, 36, 40, 79, 93
Fuzhou (Fujian province) 20

Gardens of Imagination 65–68, 74, 77–78, 86
Gas, Philippe 22, 36, 45, 50–51, 58, 69
GDP (Gross Domestic Product) 33
geopolitical risk 32
Glendale Galleria 52
Global Theme Parks Report (2015) 35, 49
Global Times 56
globalization 4, 33, 41–43, 57
glocalization 5–7, 41–43, 61, 79, 81, 87–95
Gone with the Wind 9
Good Morning, Vietnam 12
'Good Neighbor' policy 10
government relations 15, 37–43, 50, 53, 60, 85–86
Gramsci, A. 41
Grauman's Chinese Theatre 9
Great Wall 55, 72, 77–78
Greenland 72
Grizzly Gulch 19
Guangzhou (Guangdong province) 17, 20

Hall, Stuart 51–52, 73
Hangzhou (Zhejiang province) 23, 35
Hangzhou Songcheng Park 35
Hannerz, U. 42
'happiest place on Earth, the' 2
'harmonious society' 1
headquarter 16
hegemony 41, 59, 80, 84–85
heritage 24, 75
heterogeneity 86
heterogenization 40, 42
hierarchy 59
High School Musical China 55
Hollywood 8–9, 12–13, 17, 55, 89
homogeneity 42, 61
homogenization 59
Honey, I Shrunk the Kids 13
Hong Kong basic law 19
Hong Kong Disneyland: glocalization 80, 92–94; history 1–2, 13–14, 16–20, 25–26; identity

100 *Index*

47–48; ownership 30–35, 84; representation 66–71
Hong Kong International Theme Parks Limited 30
Hong Kong New Territories 18
Hong Kong Special Administrative Region (HKSRG) 16, 19, 30, 92
Hu, Jintao 1
Huayi Brothers Media Corporation 55
hybrid 94

identity 4–6, 45–52, 60, 69, 83–85, 93
ideology 58–59, 83
Iger, Robert: corporate strategy 14–5; government relation 32–33, 39; Shanghai Disneyland 20–25, 36, 41, 45, 49–51, 76, 78, 86
Iguazu waterfalls 72
imagineering 67, 72, 78
imperialism 5–6, 49–50, 71, 80; beyond 41, 58–61, 83–91, 95
in-depth interview 3
inclusion 6, 65–76, 80, 83
income 2, 10, 24, 34, 57
India 37, 39, 72
indigenization 40
infantilization 59
informant 3, 37, 51–52, 61, 68–69, 72, 74
infrastructure 23, 30, 51–52, 61, 69, 72, 74
innovation 14, 23–24, 33, 44, 74, 77, 79
Inside Out 52
inspiration 46–50
intellectual property 17, 35
interconnectedness 42
IPTV (Internet Protocol television) 54
Iron Man 19, 68
It's a Small World 71, 80

Japan 2, 31, 41, 46–47, 53, 87, 92
Japanese occupation 19
Jia Pian You Yue 1
Jiang, Zemin 39

Jiefang Daily 39
Jobs, Steve 14
joint venture: Disneyland Paris 29; Hong Kong Disneyland 19, 30; media 54; Shanghai Disneyland 4–5, 22, 31–33, 43, 83–84, 88
Journey to the West 15, 49, 75
Jungle Book, The 68
Jungle Cruise 80
Jurassic World Isla Nublar 89

Kam, Andrew 25, 34
Kang, Luke 17–18, 52–53, 58
Kansas City 8, 11
Katzenberg, Jeffery 12
keyword 4, 26, 46
Kissinger, Henry 37
Korea 18, 32, 39, 52
Kraidy, M. 42
Kundun 37–38
Kung Fu Panda Land of Awesomeness 89
Kuomintang 16

Lang, Lang 50
Lantau Island 19
Latin America 39
Lau, Samuel 25
Lee, M. 2–3, 30, 40
Lee, Xining 72
leisure time 10
Let It Go 51, 71
Li Xiusong 49
Lijiang (Yunnan province) 35
Lion King, The 13, 16, 75, 78
Little Mermaid, The 13
Local Content team 18, 52–53
local custom 43, 48
local relevance 6, 15, 52, 57, 72
localism 42
locality 7, 42, 58, 91, 93
Lucas, George 13
LucasFilm 13–14
Lujiazui 21, 53

Ma Yonghua, 32
Macau 26
Magic Kingdom Park 11

Main Street USA 11, 19, 66–67, 80
majority Chinese ownership rule 5, 31–33, 84, 89
managing director 15–17, 25, 34, 52–54
Manhattan 8
Marceline (Missouri) 11
marketing 17, 38, 41, 54
Marvel 14, 19, 35, 55–57, 68
Mary Poppins 68
MasterChef Asia 26
Matterhorn mountain 72
merchandise 2, 9, 58, 92
Mickey Avenue 65–67, 77–78
Mickey Mouse: animation 8–9, 49, 66, 70; consumer product 9, 38, 56–57, 74, 77; costume character 35, 39, 67; image 12, 15
Mickey Mouse and Donald Duck 16, 49, 53
Mickey Mouse Club, The 11, 16
Mickey Mouse Magazine 9, 16
Mickey's Storybook Express 74
middle-class 34, 58
Miller, Ronald 12
Ming Pao Daily 48
Minion Land 89
Minnie Mouse 15, 35, 48, 77
modernity 20–21, 59
Monkey King 75
Monument Valley 72
Mouseketeer 11
Mulan: animated feature 37–38, 42, 68, 70; costume character 74, 78; live-action 56, 68
Murdoch, Rupert 15
Mystic Point 19
myth 69

Nanchang (Jiangxi province) 34–35
Nanjing (Jiangsu province) 35
National Broadcasting Company (NBC) 10–11
National Bureau of Statistics of China 24–25, 67
NBA (National Basketball Association) 55
negotiation 4, 22, 36, 41, 49, 88
netizen 50, 56

New York 8–9, 12
New York World Fair 71
newspaper 16, 18, 24, 39, 48
Ning, Zetao 55
Ningbo (Zhejiang province) 20
non-disclosure agreement 4
North America 72, 91

Obama, Barack 22, 24
one country, two systems 19
One Hour in Wonderland 10
one-child policy 1, 17
opening ceremony 23–25
Opening Eve Celebration 51–52
openness 16, 20–21, 24, 33, 76, 80
Opium War 18–19
opportunity 25, 41, 61, 67, 85
oppositional reading 52, 73
organization 4–5, 41
Oriental Daily News 16
Oriental Land Co., Ltd. 29, 46, 92
Oriental Pearl Tower 72
Oswald the Lucky Rabbit 8
OTT (over-the-top) 38

P. King Duckling 39–40
parade 14, 23, 74, 78
Paramount 10, 12
Paris of Asia 21
participant observation 3
particularism 42
partnership 6, 23, 53–54, 61, 69, 84–86
Party Publicity Inc. 79
Patten, Chris 19
Paul Bunyan 67
Peking opera 18, 75, 78
People's Daily 18
Perlmutter, Isaac 14
Phoenix Legend 75
pilot 1, 19, 21, 30
Pinocchio 9
piracy 23, 35
Pirates of the Caribbean 13, 74, 78
Pixar 14, 35, 52, 65, 67
Pleasant Goat and Big Big Wolf 14
policy 1, 31, 17, 32, 37, 56, 61, 85
political economy 89–90
popular culture 3, 10, 79

population 25, 38, 54, 67
power 17, 42, 56, 59–60, 79, 90–91
Pretty Woman 13
pricing 24
primary data 3
prime time 53
Princess and the Frog, The 70
Princess Iron Fan 15
production study 3–4
promotion 13, 26, 40, 55
propaganda 10, 79
Proposal, The 55
protectionism 32–33, 37, 61, 85
protest 47, 50
proximity 18, 53, 55, 66
Pudong 21, 22, 72

Qiu, Yichuan 32
QQ Sports 55
qualitative methods 3
quota 53–54

Radio Disney 13
Ratatouille 67
Raz, A. 87
recycle 11, 40
reform 20–21, 79
regulation 4, 32, 37, 53, 83, 87, 91
relativization 91
religion 37, 53
relocalization 57
reorientation 6, 58–60
replica 35, 37, 93
representation 18, 60, 65, 79–81, 83–84, 86–89, 91–94
reputation 9, 34
research 4, 17, 24–25, 58, 69, 92
resistance 60
respect 33, 51, 69
responsive localization 80
responsive Westernization 80
restriction 53, 56
revenue sharing 16, 54
reverse imperialism 87
risk 9, 19, 29, 41, 60, 66, 93
Robertson, Roland 6, 41–42, 91
Robin Hood 68

Saludos Amigos 10
sanitization 56
SARFT (State Administration of Radio, Film and Television) 32, 53
Save Disney 14
scope 17, 31
Scorsese, Martin 37
secondary data 3
Secret of Magic Gourd, The 17, 55
Seruto, Nancy 76
Shanghai Airlines Corporation Limited, The 32
Shanghai Disney Hotel 5
Shanghai Disney Resort 22–25, 32–23, 39, 65, 74–75, 78
Shanghai Disneyland Merchandise 58
Shanghai Expo 54
Shanghai International Theme Park and Resort Management Company Limited 32–33
Shanghai International Theme Park Associated Facilities Company Limited 22, 31
Shanghai International Theme Park Company Limited 22, 31
Shanghai Media Group (SMG) 51, 54–55
Shanghai Municipal Administration of Industry and Commerce 17
Shanghai Pilot Free Trade Zone 21
Shanghai Shendi Group 5, 22, 28, 31–33, 79–80, 83–84, 88
Shanghai Stock Exchange 21
Shanghai Symphony Orchestra 51
shareholder 19, 23, 30, 81, 92
Shao, Xiaoyun 32
Shijingshan Amusement Park 35
signifier 12, 76
Silly Symphonies 68
Silly Symphony Flowers and Trees, The 9
Sister Act 13
Snow White 16, 34–35, 70
Snow White and the Seven Dwarfs 9, 15, 70
So Dear to My Heart 10
Soarin' Over The Horizon 72, 77–78
social critic 6, 50, 61, 80, 85

socialism with Chinese characteristics 2, 38, 73
soft power 56, 60, 79
Song of the South 10
Songcheng Lijiang Romance Park 35
Sony Corporation 41
Sorenson, John 67
Southeast Asia 25–26
Southern Metropolis Daily 16
Space Mountain 73, 80
Spears, Britney 11
Splendid China 35
Star Wars 14, 35, 55–56, 74
State Administration for Industry and Commerce of China (SAIC) 23
state-capital-led glocalization 5–6, 43, 61, 81, 87–93
state-led glocalization 93–94
Steamboat Mickey 66, 78
Steamboat Willie 9
Steinberg, Saul 12
stock 12–13
Stoney and Rocky 18
Stormtrooper 55–56, 74
strategy: Disney 12, 14–16, 18, 52–53, 57–58, 61; Hong Kong Disneyland 40; Shanghai Disneyland 40–41, 80, 83, 85; Sony 41
stratified localization 6, 57–58, 61, 84–85
strike 9
surface localization 20, 80
sweatshop 56–57
Switzerland 72
Sydney Opera House 72
synergy 12, 40, 74, 85

Taiwan 2–3, 26
Taj Mahal 72
Taking of Tiger Mountain, The 75
Tan, Dun 51
Tangled 68, 70
tariff 20, 32
Tarzan: Call of the Jungle 72–73, 77–78
Team Disney 12–14
technological advance 6, 40, 76–81, 86–87, 94

technoscape 79
Tencent Holdings Ltd. 36, 54
Terminal High Altitude Area Defense 32
Themed Entertainment Association 35, 49
themed land 19, 35, 46, 65–77, 80, 89, 92
Third World 59
threat 32, 46, 59, 80
Three Caballeros, The 10
Three Little Pigs, The 9
Three Men and a Baby 12–13
Tibet 37
Timberlake, Justin 11
Tokyo Disneyland: castle 69; glocalization 87, 92, 94; identity 45–48, 60; opening 2, 17; ownership 28–31; representation 66, 71, 75; strategy 20, 40
Tokyo DisneySea 13
Tomlinson, J. 59
Tomorrowland 19, 48, 65–66, 73–74, 77–78, 92
Touch of the Panda 55
Touchstone Pictures 12, 14, 37
tourism 5, 33–36, 41, 84
Toy Story 65, 68
Toy Story Hotel 65
Toy Story Land 19, 65–66, 80
trademark 23, 35, 66
transculturation 91
transformation 5, 91
Transformers: Metrobase 89
Treasure Cove 65–66, 74–78, 86
Treasure Island 10
Treaty of Beijing 18
Treaty of Huangpu 20
Treaty of Nanjing 18, 20
trial operation 39
trivialization 56
Tron 73–74, 78
True–Life Adventure series 10
Trump, Donald 32–33
Twenty-First Century Fox, Inc. 15
two-child policy 34
typology of glocalization 6, 90–94

unequal treaty 18, 20, 30
uniqueness 6, 76–78, 80, 86, 94

Universal Studios Beijing 34, 88–89
universalization 42
US–China Business Council (USCBC) 39
UYoung 39–40

violation 57

Wallerstein, I. 59
Walt Disney Company, The 12–15, 22–24, 28, 30–31, 54–55, 83, 92
Walt Disney Company (China) Limited., The 4, 6, 15–18, 52, 85–86
Walt Disney Company (Shanghai) Limited, The 17
Walt Disney Grand Theater 65, 75–76
Walt Disney Studios 7–13
Wanda City 34–35, 49
Wang, Jianlin 34, 49–50
Wang, Qingguo 32
Wang, Yang 24
Warner 12
Wasko, J. 3, 12, 79, 92
WaterWorld 89
website 11, 13–14, 16, 24, 76

Weibo 50
Wells, Frank 12
Who Framed Roger Rabbit 13
Winkler, M.J. 8
Winnie the Pooh and the Blustery Day 67–68
WiseNews 16
Wishing Star Park 65
Wizarding World of Harry Potter, The 89
Wolong Giant Panda Nature Reserve 55
World Bazaar 66
world system 59
World Trade Organization (WTO) 54, 79
World War II 10

Xi, Jinping 6, 24, 33, 36, 39, 77
Xiamen (Fujian province) 20

Yang, Xiong 23
Yangtze Delta 21

Zhu, Rongji 22
Zhuhai (Guangdong province) 35
Zootopia 55, 65